Wakefield Press

Bound for Vietnam

Believing that to travel hopefully is better than to arrive – and she sometimes almost doesn't – Lydia Laube is one of Australia's favourite travel writers. Lydia can never resist a challenge, and her books, *Behind the Veil: An Australian Nurse in Saudi Arabia*, *The Long Way Home*, *Slow Boat to Mongolia*, *Llama for Lunch*, *Temples and Tuk Tuks*, and *Is This the Way to Madagascar?*, tell of her alarming adventures in far-flung places of the globe.

When she is not travelling, Lydia Laube chases the sun between Adelaide and Darwin.

T0362934

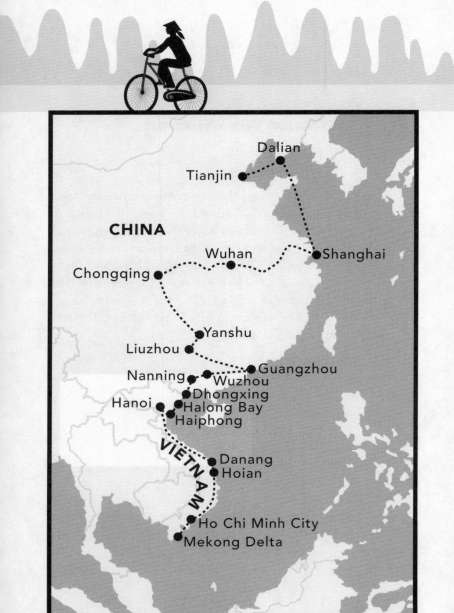

Bound for Vietnam

LYDIA LAUBE

Wakefield
Press

Wakefield Press
Box 2266
Kent Town
South Australia 5071

First published 1999
Reprinted 2007

Edited by Jane Arms
Cover designed by Nick Stewart, design BITE, Adelaide
Typeset by Clinton Ellicott, MoBros, Adelaide
Printed and bound by Hyde Park Press, Adelaide

National Library of Australia
Cataloguing-in-publication entry

Laube, Lydia, 1948– .
Bound for Vietnam.

ISBN-13: 978 1 86254 462 8.

ISBN-10: 1 86254 462 X.

1. Laube, Lydia, 1948– – Journeys. 2. Vietnam – Description
and travel. 3. China – Description and travel. I. Title.

915.9704

Government
of South Australia

Arts SA

Contents

1 A Ship for Shanghai

It's funny how life turns out when you are travelling. I had set off from Timor planning to reach China by sea, cross that country by train to Mongolia and then come home. But a chance encounter with a Welshman on the Trans-Siberian Express en route to Ulaan Bator had made me decide once again to take the long way home. I had ended up in Tianjin, a great port washed by the Bohai Sea on China's north-east coast. It sits on the banks of the Hai River, 120 kilometres from Beijing. I now planned to sail down the coast of China to Shanghai, ride riverboats as far south as I could on the Yangtze, go to Guangzhou where I had heard it was possible to get a visa for an overland crossing into Vietnam, make my way over the mountains to the border and, with luck, be allowed to enter Vietnam's far north.

The train journey from Beijing had taken me only two hours. I got off at the station with a minimum of fuss and a fellow-traveller, a Chinese man, helped me with my bags.

My guide book labelled Tianjin 'the most expensive town in China'. It was said to be a hopeless place to find a reasonably priced hotel room that was not off-limits to foreigners. Near the railway station exit I came across a table run by an official-looking woman whom I deduced, from the pictures she displayed, was selling hotel rooms. I reckoned that in these circumstances some bargaining might be in order. I asked how much. The woman wrote a figure on a piece of paper. I said, 'Too much. I only want a single room.' I wrote 200. She used a nearby public phone – there was no office, only the table – and returning said, 'Okay,' and indicated that I should go with a man she now had in tow. He turned out to be the driver of one of the little yellow vans that served as taxis. By now it was ten o'clock at night and I went willingly.

He took me to a smart hotel, where three giggling girls presided over the reception desk. They intimated that I could have a room and wrote a price: 488 yuan. I recoiled in mock horror. 'No, no,' I said, 'I can't afford that,' and began to bargain with them. We finally settled on 188 yuan.

That accomplished, it seemed to take all three young ladies forever to fill out the myriad forms that were necessary to get me admitted. And then they could not scrape up enough money to give me twelve yuan change. 'Come back tomorrow', was all they said. It's no good travelling in China without cash. You need lots of the gorgeous stuff – no one will trust you inside their establishment unless you pay up front, preferably in small denominations.

The accommodation I was finally let loose in was far above the standard to which I had become accustomed in China. And everything worked – airconditioner, lights, hot water! The toilet flushed. But there were the usual faults. The hand-basin was loose, and the shower was impossible to use; the water wouldn't mix and was either burning hot or stone cold. The young female room attendant showed me how to work everything in my room and a bell boy, the first I'd encountered on my travels, delivered and stowed my bags.

The hotel dining-room was crowded at breakfast, perhaps because the meal was included in the price of the room. The food was not riveting, but I had got up at the crack of dawn to indulge in it, so I was determined to persevere. Rice and pea gruel, which tasted like warm water that had had rice washed in it, was followed by a cold hard-boiled egg, some of the pickled cabbage I had come to like, and dumplings.

Tianjin is famous for its steamed dumplings – they are even exported to Japan – and these were delicious. There were also some strange-looking fried patties that were definitely an acquired taste – meat spread with peanut butter, sprinkled with sesame seeds and dipped in batter.

Outside the hotel, the bell boy, who was most concerned about where and how I was going, helped me get a taxi to CITS, supposedly the place to go if you need to buy tickets, or get help with your travel arrangements. CITS was located in a marvellous great building with China International Travel Service blazoned across its front. The foyer of the building was desolate except for the usual guard who sat behind a glass screen like a museum exhibit. In China I found that everyone who was exposed to the public was, wherever possible, behind barricades. Through the peephole in his glass case the guard indicated that I should state my business.

I said, 'CITS.'

He pointed upstairs, but when I took a step in that direction he said, 'No no!' He dialled a number and then handed me the phone through the aperture.

A woman asked, 'Who do you want to see?'

'No one in particular,' I said, 'I just want some help.'

'What do you want?'

'I want a ticket on a boat to Qingdoa.'

No boat went anywhere from Tianjin, she said, except for the international ferries that sailed to Korea and Japan. After this outrageous lie, Madam CITS was utterly unhelpful. She refused to admit me to the office, saying that she was not seeing anybody that day. Thinking, Funny behaviour for a firm that was in the business of helping and advising foreign visitors, I left. But the guard waved me next door to China Airlines where a beautiful young woman listened to my story and wrote down the address of the coastal boat ticket office for me.

At the shipping office the ticket-seller and I, with the aid of the phrasebook and a lot of effort, worked out where I wanted to go and how much it would cost. I went off to change some money and arrived back just before midday to discover that all the ticket windows were covered with wooden shutters. I banged on one behind which I could hear voices and was told that the office did not re-open until half past one. I sat down on the hard wooden bench to wait. An old man shuffled up and, smiling broadly at me, practised his only two words of English – both 'H' words, 'Hello and Whore'.

At a quarter to one I was joined by the first English-speaking traveller I had encountered in a long time, a Chinese named Liang. He was a friendly young man who was on holiday from his job as an electronics engineer with a French nuclear firm in Guangzhou. He decided to wait with me, and I asked him if he would help me buy my ticket. Liang was going to Dalian, and he convinced me that I should too, saying that it would be easier to get a ship to Shanghai from there than from Qingdoa.

Having eventually acquired the boat ticket, I got into a taxi intending to go to the antique market, but the driver told me that I would be wasting my money because the market closed after lunch. All the taxi drivers I encountered in this town were honest. This one took me on a much shorter trip to a local tourist attraction, the Ancient Culture Street, an area where old buildings have been restored or reproduced to recreate a traditional old town. It is centred around the Temple of the Queen of Heaven, the goddess of the sea, which dates back to 1326 AD. The buildings were impressive but the shops all sold similar souvenirs and copies of antiques that I found tedious after a while. The few genuine old pieces were either very expensive or not very good. I did buy a silk kite however, another product for which Tianjin is famous.

At the end of the Ancient Culture Street, I came to the River Hai and started walking along its bank in the direction of the city centre. It was an agreeable ramble. The river wound through the town and passed under many bridges, one of which was shaped and curved to follow the large decorative dragons that ran along each of its sides. The path by the riverside meandered under shady spreading trees and every now and then I passed small cafés that served coffee and drinks at tables and chairs in the open air.

The feeling that I was walking along the River Seine in Paris was reinforced by the ornate wrought-iron railings that edged the riverbank and which I read had been brought from France. People fished from the railings using hand lines or rods and itinerant bicycle repair, accessories and spare parts salesmen set up business beside the path. You could lean on the balustrade and watch the river while your bike was mended. Or you could perch on a tiny, three-legged stool and get your hair cut by the nomadic barber who wandered along looking for trade. Other vendors produced an instant shop by stringing a rope between two trees and hanging some goods, such as scarves, on it. One woman pedalled by on a bike that had an emporium of plastic wares and clothing dangling from its sides. At one spot I came upon a large piece of plastic sheeting that had been strung between two trees. A crowd of men behind it seemed to be gambling. It looked like a floating crap game.

The riverside railings were also used to suspend big circular fishing nets. They were attached to poles that extended outwards from a central post like the arms of an umbrella, and were hauled up and down by a winch. I watched many nets brought up but didn't see any fish in them. This caused me no grief. The river was marred by flotsam, and the town's sewerage emptied into it. I would not have wanted to eat anything that came out of it.

Strolling along under the lovely trees watching local life going by was great, but every now and then I came to a bridge, and I had to negotiate the terrifying traffic on the road that crossed it. There were lots of cars, a few carts drawn by horses or donkeys and millions of bicycles. I had learned by now that I would never get across a street if I did not just step out bravely into the bicycle brigade. I had watched how the Chinese navigated their way. The locals simply walked among the bicycles like a bunch of chooks. So, taking a deep breath I would march into the melee and rely on them to miss. They were pretty good at it too. Bikes peeled off me all around.

In Tianjin's city centre, I marvelled at a veritable architectural museum of turn-of-the-century buildings – remnants of the Europeans who had occupied segments of the town in its trading heyday. Tianjin was developed as a port and grain storage point in the fourteenth-century Yuan Dynasty following the establishment of Beijing as the Mongol capital. In 1858, the British and French invaded Tianjin, established trading posts and opened it to other countries, and the Japanese, Germans, Austro-Hungarians, Belgians and Italians also moved in. Now Tianjin has a population of five-and-a-half million people and, with two universities and numerous institutes and colleges, it is an important education centre.

The next morning I arrived at the shipping office intending to board the bus to Tanggu, fifty kilometres away, which is Tianjin's port. My friend Liang was waiting for me at the office. He persuaded me to share a taxi, saying that the bus would be overcrowded, which it was. The taxi was much more comfortable. Liang sat in the front seat with the female driver, while I reclined in the back of the van, lounging on a chintz-covered seat with my feet up like Cleopatra swanning down the Nile.

The road we travelled to Tanggu was a tangle of bikes.

They were everywhere and I was constantly surprised at how the taxi managed to miss them. We drove over many of the canals and waterways that crisscross Tianjin and on their landscaped edges, as well as in the frequent leafy parks, I saw people doing tai chi and grandparents minding children; one elderly man was teaching a small boy to ride a tricycle along a canal path.

Once outside the city, however, we were in a dreary industrial landscape that was only relieved by an occasional, unintentionally humorous sign. I saw one that proclaimed a building to be 'The Long Smooth Perfect Article Factory'. I am still wondering what exactly they made. They certainly weren't giving away any such information before you got in the door, but any time I want a long smooth perfect article, I shall know where to go.

The only other interesting sight on the highway was a mule train; a team of ten heavily loaded mules plodded along amid the zooming traffic.

Tanggu seemed to consist mainly of low sailors' dives. There were whole streets of them, presumably catering to the droves of Chinese tourists who land here by ship from Macau and Hong Kong. I remembered my friends, the seamen of the Good Ship *Pandora*, with whom I had once hitched a ride across the Indian Ocean and who had promised to show me a low sailors' dive in Bombay. This had never eventuated, and I am still waiting for this elevating experience to enrich my life.

Liang and I lunched in a wharf-side café that had poor food at inflated prices. Our ship, the *Tiansin*, carried 500 passengers, but it was not overcrowded. The toilets, however, were the communal trough and trench variety, but without running water, and so they came complete with piles of other people's doings.

As the *Tiansin* pulled out of port, I made for the bow of the ship where I could see a sole occupant. On closer inspection I heard loud retchings and heavings, which explained his solitude. I left him to it.

I had only been able to buy a second-class ticket on the *Tiansin*, and I found myself in a four-bunk cabin with three young men for company. What a good conversation opener that would make. 'I spent the night between Tianjin and Dalian with three young men!' The cabin was large and functional, but it had no privacy. The door even contained an eye-level, uncurtained window through which anyone who had a mind to could peer in at you from the passageway. It reminded me of the windows in the doors of prison cells that are used for checking on the inmates.

That evening Liang and I ate together in the ship's huge cafeteria. We had a cheap meal of chicken that was a minefield of small bones which my dinner companion spat directly onto the tablecloth. A big brown bottle of beer cost me three yuan – twenty-four cents – but came without anything in the line of a drinking vessel. At intervals during dinner I clutched this huge bottle by the neck and swigged out of it, imagining how such niceties would go down in polite society.

Later I wandered around the deck. The sea was like dark-green glass and the ship made hardly any movement as it slid over it. In the cabin I lay on my upper bunk and watched the ocean through the port-hole. My room-mates had all fallen on their beds the minute they had come aboard ship and slept until dinner time, after which they had prepared for bed and slept again, snoring, until morning. Except for two of them, who had woken at about ten in the evening and begun smoking and talking. Then one had started to sing softly. It must have been a lullaby, because I went to sleep.

At eleven the next morning, the *Tiansin* slid slowly past a long breakwater and tied up at the wharf of Dalian. We had been a good while coming into this massive and busy harbour. Crowded with ships, its docks lined by imposing warehouses, it reminded me of Bombay. Overshadowing the warehouses were huge cranes that worked away, picking things up and putting them down frantically like giant, stick-insect robots gone mad. And over everything hung a heavy grey pall of pollution.

I went ashore, disappointed that I had not seen Liang this morning. I feared his desertion might have been brought on by my questions. I had noticed that he did not ask me anything personal. Was this because he was too polite? Perhaps he had thought I was a spy. Perhaps he was the spy! He had told me that his job as an electronics engineer at the French company's nuclear station in South China involved the disposal of toxic waste materials. I had been shocked at his reply to my question, 'What do you do with it?' In a matter of fact manner, he simply said, 'We put it in the sea.'

I had also asked him how he felt about the new path that China was taking. He said that he did not like to see the old culture destroyed, but he liked some things. 'Like discos?' I asked. 'Yes,' he answered, smiling. 'You mean you want to keep some of the old ways, but the freedom is good.' I said, and he agreed. Maybe it had been the word 'freedom' that had scared him off. It is a new concept in China. Or it could have been that he was deterred by the thought of a re-encounter with the clunky luggage that he had had to help me carry on board.

A hike along the wharf brought me to the place where buses waited to ferry passengers to the terminal exit. I stood back, confounded, while two buses were stampeded until they were full and left. Eventually the sheer number of Chinese behind me propelled me onto a bus. I rode standing in a solid press of bodies and hanging on to the back of a seat for grim death.

Disgorged into the street, I found myself in front of a great flight of steps which I thought led to the shipping terminal offices where I might buy a ticket to Shanghai. I struggled up this monumental obstacle course to discover that it wasn't so. I lumped my bags further down the road. It was lined by offices that could possibly have been travel agents, so I stepped into one to enquire. An obliging man went to find someone who spoke English and shortly charming Miss Fong materialised. She made a phonecall for me and informed me that the boat would leave the next day. Miss Fong directed me to the ticket office, a cavernous affair a few doors down. Here I waited patiently while a woman meticulously stamped and sorted thirty thousand tickets under the enthralled gaze of the cluster of people who pressed about her. Although it was obvious that nothing was happening up front, the woman behind me wouldn't stand quietly and kept pushing me closer and closer until she eventually wormed her way up alongside me in the starting gates. But I got shunted up to the desk before she managed to pass me.

The ticket lady made it known to me that Miss Fong had been wrong – there were no tickets to Shanghai. All the people behind me joined in the effort of deciphering the phrasebook. 'No ticket to Shanghai,' they chorused.

I returned to Miss Fong and said that perhaps the ticket seller had not understood me. She very kindly dropped what she was doing, locked her desk and went to see for herself. Fifteen minutes later she returned and said, 'Sorry, no tickets today. You try tomorrow.'

She dialled a number and let me speak to a man who explained that it was not possible to buy a ticket in advance. You had to get to the ticket office when it opened at eight o'clock in the morning and fight for a ticket for that day.

My guidebook claimed that there was a baggage storage office in the vicinity, but it proved elusive. I suspect that it was secreted in the International Terminal Building, but a large policeman barred the entrance and sent me packing.

I wasn't allowed in there without a ticket to prove I was going somewhere.

A taxi driver with a little English accosted me. I explained that I wanted a hotel that wasn't too dear and we set off on the big search for this rare animal. Dalian was reputed to run a close second to Tianjin in the Most Expensive race. At the first hotel the driver and I discussed the price I would pay and he went in to negotiate for me – to no avail. Three hotels and a similar amount of rejections later, he finally established me in the Fortune Hotel at a cost of 220 yuan a night.

The Fortune Hotel was another of those places where I was not allowed the responsibility of a key. The room attendant came attached at the waist to a thousand keys that jangled on a lump of fencing wire fixed to a railway sleeper. She rattled up and down the wire through a cacophony of keys until she found the one that matched my door. And each time I went in or out the door I had to find her to lock or unlock it for me.

A sign over the front entrance of the hotel claimed that it had a restaurant. When I asked the desk staff to direct me to it, I was marched to the front door and handed to the doorman, a severe-looking fellow who turned out to be most amiable. Taking me in his custody, he trundled me down the street, across the road and into a place that served Chinese fast food. The doorman dragged me all around the room pointing out the food on the tables and the pictures of it on the walls, before giving me into the keeping of a young man at the counter.

I ate some luscious steamed dumplings that were filled with a kind of green spinach and shrimps. I had been determined not to touch anything out of these polluted waters, but it was delicious. Seafood was the gastronomic specialty of Dalian, and it was hard to avoid it. Local tourists flock here to eat it, seemingly unconcerned by the foul state of the ocean it comes from. A dish of tasty sauce that contained at least six cloves of garlic accompanied each serve – with any luck it would kill any lurking bacteria. My attendant/keeper brought me a special serviette and a spoon, rather than chopsticks, and looked after me very well – all for the cost of a dollar. When I prepared to leave, he took me, literally, by the hand, and led back me to the hotel. And not just to the door, but right into the foyer. I must look mentally defective, I thought.

Later, in my girlish innocence – or stupidity – I again tried CITS. I thought they would help me to get a ticket to Shanghai. I never learn! The phone was answered by someone who spoke no English and hung up on me. Totally disillusioned with CITS, I gave it away.

We had crossed the Bohai Sea to reach Dalian, which is situated on the tip of the Liaoning Peninsular of Manchuria in China's north east. Dalian is an important port with a buoyant economy and a busy industrial centre. Occupied by the Japanese in the late nineteenth century, it became a Russian concession, known as Luda, in 1898. Dalian was a valuable asset to the Russians and they planned to make it their great warm-water port. But, after the Russo-Japanese war in 1905, it was taken from them again by the Japanese. The Soviet Union re-claimed Dalian after the second world war and kept it for ten years – until Chinese liberation.

There is a feeling of prosperity in Dalian's wide cobblestone streets, but although it has long been a summer resort for Chinese, few western faces are seen here. Russian smugglers are said to be the usual foreign visitors. I had not seen a westerner for ages. Not that I wanted to; most of them were an embarrassment. I didn't realise how ugly we could be until I passed one on the street in Dalian, and, looking at him through unfamiliar eyes saw him as the Chinese must have done. No wonder they stare. I did too. With his peaky, rat face, extremely pale and blotchy skin, tatty mouse brown hair and grotty clothes, he looked very strange indeed.

Dalian's buildings are an eclectic medley of architectural styles; Chinese, Japanese, old Russian and new Soviet mingled with fabulous, massive old colonial buildings. In the main square there is even a copy of a Bavarian castle. The old Russian and Japanese-built bourgeois suburbs survive today as seedy semi-detached villas with brick walls, bungalows with picket fences and big churches that are used as schools and municipal buildings.

Dalian was a pleasant surprise. Like Tianjin it was more westernised than other Chinese cities I had visited. It was also cleaner, the traffic was not as horrendous and there were fewer bikes. And the people I had come across had been friendly. Some of them were natty dressers too. Although people looked at me, no one screamed, 'Loala' – foreigner – or 'Gweilo' – foreign devil – in my face. And I actually found my way downtown and back from the hotel on foot – alone and unaided!

I wandered into a bank to ask if they changed money. The teller said, 'Upstairs'. 'Upstairs' denied this, but it had been worth the climb. The white marble staircase had an onyx hand-rail that imitated malachite and from the mezzanine floor I had a good view of this very beautiful building. A young employee left her desk and took me to a plate glass window to point out the street I should go down to find another bank.

In the next bank, another stunning building that had walls covered with glittering mosaics and a jade fountain in the centre of the black marble floor, I changed some money with an amiable young man who came out from behind his counter to practise his English with me. A tall, distinguished-looking Chinese nearby asked the teller what nationality I was. 'Ah,' he exclaimed with delight, 'Otraylia! Where have you come from in Otraylia?' 'Darwin.' I replied, thinking that he would never have heard of it, or anywhere else except Sydney, for that matter. But to my complete surprise he said, 'I have just come from Geralton. And Bunbury. I am captain of ship. We take minerals.'

'Fabulous,' I said, 'You don't take passengers too, do you?' He laughed and said no. 'What a shame,' I replied, 'I am looking for a ship to Shanghai.'

Later I found the Friendship Store, but I was disappointed. The same goods were far cheaper in Hong Kong. It was on the staircase of this shop that I made a firm resolve never to touch another hand-rail in China. I saw a man blow his nose with his fingers, flick the proceeds onto the stairs and then wipe his hand on the rail.

I went across the street to visit the International Seamans' Club. It was splendid. It even had its own post office with an international computer-controlled pay phone. A much better arrangement than in the government telephone office in Beijing where I had been hit for an enormous amount of money: no one had let me know how long I had been speaking.

Returning to my hotel, I discovered that at about five o'clock in the evening the veggie market in the street outside blossomed into a night market that extended into many of the surrounding streets. I love night markets. They are always vibrant; and ordinary everyday things take on a festive air when they are displayed under rows of lights strung like fairy lanterns against the canvas backs of tiny stalls. I spent a couple of hours rummaging happily through the wares.

2 VIP Voyage

I awoke in Dalian to the sound of rain on the window-ledge. It was the first good steady rain I had seen in a long time. I was on the footpath outside the hotel by half past seven in the morning – some sort of miracle for me. The streets were almost deserted except for the cleaners who, covered by long, black waterproof capes and with black hoods over their heads, looked like glistening ants wielding stick brooms and pushing wooden carts about.

I was the second person to front the rails at the Shanghai boat ticket window, but before long I was surrounded, and, if I had not seized the counter like a drowning woman clutching a spar of driftwood, I would shortly have been on the tail end of a long queue. Instead of lining up in the sheep-dip like rails that were supposed to promote an orderly line, the crowd struggled five deep along the edge of the counter, ready to create pandemonium the minute the ticket seller arrived.

Although I was the second person served, I was told that there were no first-class tickets left. There's something funny here, I thought. If tickets are issued each day and I am the first to ask for one, where are today's tickets? Obviously someone was rorting the system. 'Come back tomorrow,' the official said. But that was what she had said yesterday. I refused to budge. To get rid of me the ticket seller offered me a second-class ticket for the ship leaving that afternoon. I took it.

Back in the hotel I packed, ruefully surveying my sodden jeans. I had washed them thinking that I'd be leaving tomorrow. The sound of building work reverberated all around. The hotel was being renovated. Despite its three star status, my room was a masterpiece of bungling. All the bathroom fittings were chipped, the towel rails clung precariously to the walls, the taps could only be turned off with great difficulty, and the drain hole in the sink had no covering grate – I lost the soap the first time I used it. The electrical plugs looked extraordinarily dangerous. They drooped, with exposed wires, not quite fastened to the walls, from uneven holes. The window was cracked and didn't quite shut, or open, and the usual, almost obligatory, stains adorned the carpet.

Walking the length of the domestic ship terminal, I felt it might go on forever. As big as six large railway stations, it looked suspiciously Russian-built.

Halfway along the terminal I came upon a jolly old man in a white coat. Beaming, he held out a wooden tray covered with an assortment of sea-sickness pills for my inspection. A marvellous touch for those with suggestive minds. Stallholders sold the usual edibles; boring looking buns, red-clad sausages, bottles of beer and wine, lurid lolly water and millions of cigarettes. One extensive stall that sold mostly unwrapped comestibles was positioned smack against a large public toilet.

Installed in the waiting area indicated for my ship, I found it was cold, damp and draughty in this big open place. And being so near the water made it worse. The rain of the morning had stopped, but after a while – as soon as there was a distinct possibility that I might have to drag my bags through it to reach the ship – it started again. Although I had arrived at the terminal the requested two hours before take-off time, a crowd was already in situ when I got there.

This one was eating, spitting, yelling and carrying on. Opposite me an old man in a Mao cap and suit dozed, his gnarled, leathered hands folded in his lap. But his wife, an ancient crone weather-beaten to the colour of a ripe walnut, stared at me in amazement. The bloke next to me unblinkingly watched everything I did. Unashamedly turning sideways in his chair so as not to miss anything, his eyes followed every move I made. Plastic spittoons had been placed enticingly here and there, but most people ignored them and spat on the floor. An attentive father held his infant over one, however, so that it could pee into it through its strategically split pants.

After a time, several uniformed women walked among the seats examining tickets. I was sent to wait with a small bunch of passengers who, seated directly in front of the turnstile that led onto the wharf, were secluded from the common herd. I supposed that this was to enable us to get a head start in the marathon race onto the ship. The excluded mob stood up and, growling their discontent, glowered at us from over the other gate. But, despite the handicapper's favouritism, as soon as we were out of the starting gates the mob caught up with, and passed me.

The moment I stepped outside the waiting area the rain came down harder. I sloshed through deep puddles along the wharf until I came to three flights of steps. I cursed. At the bottom of the steps buses waited to convey the passengers to the ship and once more the crowd fought frantically to get in.

I was finally shoved onto a bus. It trundled along in the now teeming rain and deposited me on the wharf in front of the ship. Before I made it up the gangplank and under shelter, I had to cross a wide open space where I was stopped three times by police who wanted to see my ticket, passport or anything else that I could provide for them to play with.

'American?' I was asked.

'No, Australian.'

'OK.'

I think they were just curious, but in the pouring rain? I was drenched by the time I had been pushed and propelled up the gangplank.

On the ship from Tianjin to Dalian I had discovered that, although I had been told there were no first-class cabins, there were actually plenty of empty ones on the ship. So now, when I was joined in the cabin allotted to me by three young men who were pleasant and personable, but who were all smoking heavily, I decided to ask if I could upgrade.

I approached the ship's officer, who had helped me carry my bags up the last few stairs. He was a real Creepy Drawers. I found his appearance and manner repulsive: Danny de Vito on a bad day – bulging eyes of evil aspect, heavy brows and thick lips. And he touched me. In China I had been pushed, shoved, and man-handled more in a short space of time than I had ever been before, but I had not been touched in an offensive manner. Creepy Drawers spoke slyly to me in Chinese, which sounded as though he was insinuating something. And when the young men joined me in the cabin, he came in and leered at me.

After I asked if I could change to a first-class cabin, Creepy went away and returned with a young woman who spoke some English. I wasn't sure whether she understood what I wanted, but I watched her, Creepy and another uniformed officer have a long discussion. Then she said, very politely, 'Please wait,' and returned shortly with a colossal bundle of keys.

'Come and look.'

After many attempts to open a glass-fronted door which none of the keys seemed to fit, she gave up, went to the other side of the ship and finally got the corresponding door open. Inside was what looked like a board room that stretched all the way across the prow. It contained a convention of chairs, a television set and one huge 1960s wooden table. For a moment I thought I was about to be billeted in here, but, no, a door led off one side wall which, after much more struggling with keys (I deduced that these rooms were not used much) opened onto a large cabin suite. One corner was occupied by a capacious double bed which Creepy took some pains to point out to me. Every time he came in afterwards, and this was often, he eyed the bed, looking at it longingly. I wondered, a little apprehensively, if he had deliberately arranged this secluded site in order to separate me from the mob, like a dingo separates a sheep from the flock before it pounces.

For all that I was delighted with my new accommodation and gladly paid the extra fee.

From my cabin's big portholes that looked down on the ship's prow, I saw a few hardy souls brave the rain that continued to fall steadily and come out on deck as the ship left port. Not me. I was for comfort. Cosy in my special nest, I watched the ship sail through the two arms of the breakwater that encircled the harbour. Although it was only two in the afternoon, it was already so dark that the light beacons on the breakwaters were flashing. The face of the sea was heavily pitted by raindrops, but its grey surface was only disturbed by small, even risings. The sky was as grey as the sea and where they met it was so shrouded in mist that it was hard to see where one began and the other left off.

At first Creepy and the other attentive crew member kept popping in with towels, hot water for the thermos, and other luxuries. I thought they'd never stop looking after me. But finally the girl said, 'Now you rest,' and I was alone to survey my splendour, and to wonder whether at any moment I would discover that the cabin actually belonged to Creepy. The thought then struck me that he had the keys.

One of the first things I noticed was the absence of a spittoon. Almost all the accommodation I had occupied so far had been adorned with one, usually an enamelled tin job that looked like an old-fashioned potty.

The *Ningxia* was Chinese-built and about the same 1950s vintage as the *Hai Sing*, the ship on which I had travelled from Hong Kong to Shanghai. But this vessel had been designed for local, not international, use and was very different. The *Ningxia* carried 800 passengers-some of whom travelled on her decks. Her exterior sported considerable rust and paint was conspicuously absent, but her interior boasted laminated wooden bulkheads and doors and the blond wooden furniture that was popular in the fifties and sixties in Australia. Overall there was a lack of finish to the fittings and all work seemed incomplete and grotty.

My cabin, however, was as big as you would get in a state-room on the QE2. It had a good red carpet, the first unstained carpet I had seen in China, and several iron-framed portholes that did not seem to have been opened in years; the screw bolts on either side were rusted solid. The attractive edging around the portholes had been roughly tacked on, but this fault was hidden by red velvet curtains. The big double bed that was the object of Creepy's affec-tions was set cozily in an alcove between two wardrobes and dark red velvet curtains could be pulled across it to form a snug nook. Patterned tiles decorated the nook's ceiling and a porthole at the foot of the bed meant that I could sit up first thing in the morning and look at the sea. Against the bulkhead rested two blankets that had been art-fully folded into the shape of lotus flowers. There was even a reading light, but it didn't work. Not that I really thought it would.

A dark-blue, vinyl couch was fixed to the bulkhead under a porthole on the other side of the cabin. Alongside it two comfy armchairs were separated by a laminex topped table complete with a two foot high plastic bonsai tree in a stand that looked about as genuine as a green plastic Christmas tree. There was a wall-mounted electric fan that worked! But the desk light didn't, neither did the radio attached to the wall – the knob had seized. Ditto the wall clock. Beside an ample desk a metal rack fixed to the bulkhead held the omnipresent thermos and cup.

The bathroom was very rusty, the ceiling was water stained, the light didn't work and the usual plumbing repairs were necessary, but it contained a submarine deep bath, which was clean! and mobs of wonderful hot water. The toilet seat was a clunky, wooden model that looked indestructible and a large wooden letterbox held the toilet paper. An intermittent soughing noise, like the sound of waves in the sea, came out of the loo, and the water in it sloshed rhythmically back and forth. This sound increased in proportion to the speed or motion of the ship and when you sat on the toilet you were treated to a cold updraft every now and then, which was mildly disconcerting.

My cabin's position on the highest point of the ship's prow made it utterly private, a novelty in China and a wonderful change. I was contentedly resting as bid when, at a quarter to five, two young ladies called to tell me it was supper-time. Because I was in the VIP room, I was treated like one for the entire voyage. I was made the number one pet of the crew and pandered to like royalty. It became quite embarrassing. The thought occurred to me that if Mao had travelled on this ship, he would have occupied this cabin; the bed I was sleeping in was the bed he would have slept in.

The two young ladies escorted me through the hungry-looking horde that was kept waiting outside the door of the empty dining room until I was seated. Then they fussed over me like the VIP that I had suddenly and mysteriously become, as they tried to discover what I would like to eat.

I said, 'I will eat anything you bring,' much to their amusement. Just then a waiter dumped a styrofoam food receptacle containing a heap of wet wooden clothes pegs on the table. 'But I won't eat that!' I said. Gales of giggles.

What I did eat was great; some sort of chopped spiced meat. I had no idea what, and I hoped it wasn't one of the local exotica. At least I knew it couldn't be rat. I had just read how Dalian folk had recently completed a successful campaign to exterminate their rodents.

I sat on a small wooden stool at a rough wooden table to dine. Windows all around the large room opened onto the deck. The glass was missing from the one in front of my table, so I got a good stiff breeze in my face to accompany my meal. The wooden peg mystery was eventually solved. Your order was placed in a peg that had the number of your table written on it. And you did not get your nose inside a feed bag unless you had paid in full, up front. In one corner of the dining room, a man seated behind a wooden bench sold large bottles of warm beer. Qingdoa beer, the best in China, was seven yuan – about eighty cents. I don't mind room temperature beer when the weather is as cold as it was up there, off the coast of Manchuria.

When I had finished eating, my two escorts took me back to my cabin and invited me to dance in the restaurant at seven. I put on my dancing shoes. The restaurant turned out to be the grotty dining room thinly disguised. The main lights had been dimmed, a ring of coloured lights surrounded a cleared central area and a karioke had been set up in one corner. (Where some absolutely dreadful singing went on.) Creepy was seated at the door flanked by two muscled henchman, who were punching back would-be boarders like the heroes in a swashbuckling pirate film. A ticket was obviously needed for admission. I did not have one, but this omission was overlooked. No drinks were served, but your ticket entitled you to a carton of soy milk.

A young couple sat down next to me and started a conversation. Creepy asked me to dance and as I was brought up never to refuse to dance with a gentleman unless he was dead drunk, I submitted. We did a sedate sort of fox trot around the floor. Then one of the girls asked me. It was a first for me to waltz with a woman. I am not too keen to repeat it either. There was no rock and roll on this coastal ship, as there had been on the *Hai Sing*, but there was a bit of disco. These frenetic Saturday-night revels ended early and abruptly. At twenty-five past eight the lights were thrown on and a general fast exodus erupted.

I went to bed with a book, luxuriating in the best bed I had encountered on these travels. Encased in my wooden surrounds, I felt cocooned and warm. During the night I was awakened by the sound of something slamming rhythmically. I felt the ship rolling and knew that we had left the shelter of the bay and entered the open sea.

By daylight the roll had increased, and I got out of bed to a steady lift and swell. The sun came up on a dark blue empty sea that had a few white-caps on it, but nothing else in sight. I had a wonderful bath in brown (I hope it was only rust from the pipes) water. Sitting in liquid up to my chin that tipped and dipped and sloshed with the movement of the ship, I had waves without even moving.

I was left to spend a peaceful morning alone until eleven o'clock when I was again collected and escorted to a meal. My new friends from last night joined me. He was a doctor of medicine, she was a biologist, and they were part of a group on their way to Shanghai for a conference. I think Cupid had struck. This pleased me, as they made a happy couple.

After lunch, the sun came out. It lay on my book as I wrote at the desk and patterned the carpet at my feet with the shape of the windows. All day we headed steadily south through a moderate swell. The weather became warmer and the sky cleared to a bright blue. That evening I walked around the deck. It was still warm and now it was so calm that the breeze hardly ruffled my hair. The sea remained wide and empty. We had passed only an occasional freighter going the other way. As dusk closed the day, dark gunmetal storm clouds, tinged pink at their edges, gathered. A passing container ship showed a light on the blackening expanse of the ocean and the clouds became screens for furnaces of fire.

That evening I was escorted to the feeding station and helped to dine again, but fast! It was hard not to bolt your food when people stood three deep at your elbow waiting for your seat.

I was woken at two the next morning by the decreasing of the ship's roll and on looking out of the porthole I saw the lights of the Shanghai River in the distance. Shortly after three, we entered the channel of the river. Far away on each side fairy lights glowed that came closer together later as the river narrowed. It was very pretty, but I would rather have been asleep. At five there was a knock on the door. The young biologist had been brought by an officer to tell me to be ready to disembark at half past. We were to be escorted off first. My VIP status had now rubbed off on my two friends. More embarrassment! We three sat in the empty dining room watching the sun slowly turn the sky pink and light the buildings and ships that we slipped past.

At six o'clock we passed under the suspension bridge and edged up to the dock. My bags were carried off the ship by a steward and with the help of my friends I was bundled into a taxi.

I went to the Pujiang, the hotel I had stayed at on my previous visit to Shanghai. Here there was, as usual, no room at the inn. I left my bags in their care and went next door to the Shanghai Mansions for a very expensive, and meagre, breakfast. But I had the unmitigated pleasure of watching a family of four Chinese struggle to use knives and forks to eat their bacon and eggs. These were the first eating irons I had seen in a long while. The family held a piece of cutlery in each fist and tried to pick up their food as though they were tongs – a messy and not very successful operation. Meanwhile behind me there was a familiar slurping noise, which I took for granted to be a Chinese enjoying his gruel, until I discovered it came from an underwater vacuum cleaner that was being used to clean out the fish tank.

Returning to the Pujiang to wait for a room, I sat in the foyer and chatted to an Australian couple who had two delightful kids in tow. After an hour they left seeking beds elsewhere, but I persisted in my vigil until after checkout time at twelve noon when I was told that there were no spaces in four-bed rooms. I was asked if I would take a single room instead. Would I what! The existence of this rare phenomenon had always been hotly denied in the Pujiang. I had been told that they never had any, not now, not ever. But the last time I had been here, only a few weeks ago, they'd had a restaurant serving breakfast. Now all knowledge of dining rooms and food was refuted, but the single room had appeared. I gave up on this puzzlement. Perhaps the restaurant had been converted into single rooms.

My room turned out to be located on a floor way up in the Gods that must have been the former servants' quarters. The lift and grand staircase ended at the fifth floor below it and from there you ascended a set of dark, steep stairs to the attic. I imagined the ghosts of weary maid-servants trudging up these stairs late at night.

Most of the rooms on my floor were empty, but it was a good thing I did not have a lot of company. The polished wooden boards creaked and shook when anyone walked, or thundered, down the passage past my door. I turned on the television. The picture was heavily frosted, but Margot Fonteyn and Rudolf Nureyev were dancing 'Swan Lake'.

Later it produced Dan Daily and Ernest Borgnine sprouting high-pitched, choppy Mandarin in a 1950s Hollywood musical extravaganza. I eventually worked out how to get the desk lamp to stay on. It only functioned when the switch was placed alongside the cupboard and the table squeezed up against it.

One drawback to living in the attic was that the bathroom I had to use was three flights of stairs down on the third floor. I had to dash back up the main staircase with dripping hair, clutching my dressing gown and sponge bag to my chest as I passed respectably clad people going out for the day. The bathroom, in an annexe off the side of the building, was a dingy old square room covered all over in white tiles and with drainage holes in the floor that made it look like a gas chamber. The floor sloped away a good four inches as though the annexe was sliding down the outer wall. It felt as though I was still on the ship. Ancient pipes ran down the walls to two antique taps that spouted a solid jet of water which, without the refinement of a shower rose, pelted you from an overhead pipe. I got a drenching torrent of stone cold water and beat a hasty retreat. Ten minutes later it was still running cold, so I sought help. A housemaid said she would come and show me how to get hot water. I took off my clothes again, put them on the bench on one side of the bathroom and was standing there nude and freezing when she came in and said, 'You wait.' She removed her shoes, turned both the taps on full bore and latched the door open. I was on public view again. Then, to my amazement the maid calmly dropped her trousers, whipped off her shirt and joined me in the shower.

This day was the first clear day I had seen in Shanghai. It was Monday and the factories had been shut for the weekend. The line of spectacular nineteenth-century buildings along the Bund, Shanghai's famous riverfront, stood out against a blue sky. I was glad I saw Shanghai in this light. It was also fantastic to be warm enough to throw off my woollies, even though the locals were out buying their longjohns and the shops were full of winter fashions.

Feeling the need to pig out on something uncomplicated, I walked to Nanning Street to disgrace myself at McMaggot's with two Big Macs and a Coke. I wouldn't be caught dead in a place like this at home. Sometimes in China, though, it was a welcome relief to eat something so utterly, familiarly western.

At the river-boat office, just off the Bund, I managed to buy a ticket on the boat leaving that night for Wuhan. I would be able to change vessels there and go on to Chungking, which was almost as far as river passenger transport went. I walked back along the Bund, past the harbour and across Huangpu Creek, to the Pujiang. Styrofoam containers choked the creek and the edges of the river. On the bridge an old woman, who looked about the same age as her wares, sold hundred-year eggs from a wicker push cart.

3 River Dragons

At five in the evening I went to the riverboat terminal on
the Bund. Boarding the steamer presented no problems,
except that in this huge place there was no sign to tell me
which ship left from where. I showed my ticket to several
people stationed at gateways and sat in a waiting area I
hoped was the right place. I allowed a porter to carry
my bags aboard, more as an act of charity than from
necessity.

The big riverboats were better than the coastal ships.
They carried about 700 passengers who were mostly accommodated in cabins that housed ten to twenty people. The
entire bottom deck of the boat held cargo, and only a
few people travelled deck class or slept in the corridors.
Officially there was no first class – the top-ranking category
was called 'second' as a concession to communist sensitivity.
But in the isolation of the prow and away from the smelly,
crowded areas, it was still exclusive. Third class was on the
other end of the same deck and the hoi polloi were on the
two lower decks. A guard, stationed on a chair at the
entrance to the second-class section, repelled invaders from
the lesser ranks. A big notice like a stop sign stood beside
him. I supposed it said, 'Peasants keep out!'

I found myself sharing a two-bed cabin on the outside
deck with a back-packing British female with no hair. The
cabin beds had curtains that could be pulled around them
for privacy. On one wall was a vinyl bench seat and, on the

other, a small mirror-fronted cupboard hung above a wash basin whose taps produced brown river water.

This ship, the *Yangtze Star*, was the cleanest conveyance I had travelled on so far in China. But there was the usual hawking and spitting all around. I always put my head out over the deck railing very warily. You could cop more than a face full of fresh air out there. The well-bred spat over the side, the ill-mannered, on the deck. But the decks and cabin floors were washed down frequently and the Western toilets in second class were swabbed out now and then. I was to find that other riverboats were also reasonably clean, which was a wonder after the filthy coastal ships, but their toilets usually suffered due to the inability of the locals to use them or flush them in the western way. Some Chinese relieved themselves how and when they liked. Through the door of a toilet which he had, with a singular lack of modesty, left wide open, I saw one man peeing on the floor. Another I caught unconcernedly spraying overboard.

The *Yangtze Star* set off down the Huangpu River in the dark. The lights that strung out along the Bund looked sensational. It was fairyland. Shanghai's pride and joy, the garish TV tower, with its iridescent pink and green lights, resembled something out of a Disney movie – lurid, sensational, and unbelievable. The shore lights gradually became further apart as we moved downriver making for the place where the Huangpu joins the mouth of the Yangtze, China's longest river, at the sea. A dark junk slid past, outlined between us and the shore. Lit only by a dim lantern, it was an Oriental vignette. Many big boats towing barges on long chains also passed us, as well as small craft of all kinds – sampans, fishing boats and dugouts. Nothing was smart or new, and I saw no pleasure craft. The boats that were mostly used as work-horses on the river were long and narrow and had a wheel-house perched on their rear ends and open decks in front where cargo was carried.

There were a few lights on the riverbanks far away as we passed around the island in the middle of the confluence of the two rivers and turned into the wide Yangtze channel.

My room-mate, Susan, was going home to England via Beijing after working for a year in Japan. We investigated the boat and found no one on the staff who spoke a word of English and few facilities. There was a dining room of sorts, but most passengers bought meals that were dispensed in plastic boxes, all of which went overboard when they had finished. On one side of the ship a vendor sold fruit from boxes and, of all the curious things to find on a boat like this, a clothing stall had been set up on one of the companionways between decks. Here, amid much hilarity, I allowed Susan and the shop lady to convince me that I could not live without a pair of gold, yellow and black striped silk pants. I put the pants on and modelled them, much to their delight. It was the only time I ever wore them. Once off the boat I thought they were dreadful. I also bought a pair of knickers with a zippered pocket in front. For money? But how did you get to it when it was wanted?

It soon became cold outside on the river, but it was warm and cosy in our cabin. Next-door we had noisy neighbours who shouted at the top of their voices, bumped the walls and slammed their door with absolute abandon. At times during the night we stopped at towns. The engines would shut down and the racket next door would start up again to mingle with the noise from the wharf and the stamping of heavy feet overhead where the bridge and crew quarters were.

At dawn I looked out to see the immense, muddy brown waters of the Yangtze on which, partly shrouded by a grey mist, the river traffic meandered. A cold wind blew onto the deck and occasional whitecaps broke on the water. We stopped at a dreary riverside town where I watched a dredge working and a man on the deck of a pontoon below wash his longjohns and shirt in a tin basin and hang them on a conveniently strung rope.

After half an hour the boat's hooter gave a loud blast and we were off again. The *Yangtze Star*, for all its size and appearance of being top heavy, took off smartly from landings and rapidly gathered speed.

The Yangtze River is known as Chang Jiang, the long river. And so it is. It is the third longest river in the world, and is beaten only by the Nile and the Amazon. Arising in the snow-covered Tanggulashan mountains in Qinghai, it flows through Tibet and cuts across the middle of China through seven provinces, before emptying into the East China Sea near Shanghai. The voyage from Shanghai to Chongqing takes at least eight days.

At first the riverbanks were out of sight, one or two kilometres away. Later the river became less immense. It was still very wide, but the trees and greenery on its banks could be seen occasionally. By mid-morning, passing kilometres of smoke stacks and grey buildings, we came to the large city of Nanjing. This was the ancient capital of China and has a recorded history that dates back to the Warring States Period in 476 BC. Here the sluggish brown river was crossed by a good-looking bridge, which our boat pulled to one side to pass under as though the captain knew the channel well. This impressive double-story bridge – road on top, rail below – is one of the world's longest.

After Nanning, rice paddies and rushes lined the muddy shore from which now and then rows of green fishing nets protruded, while men in small boats fished close to the banks with nets that stuck out in semi-circles from their sides. Behind the paddy fields trees marched to the skyline. On the two or three stops we made during the day I took the opportunity to pound across the barges that were used as pontoons and landings and investigate the riverbank stalls that sold supplies to passengers. Here I obtained beer, Coke (or a reasonable imitation of it), the pickled eggs that I had developed a taste for when I had got past their appearance, and other essential provisions. Once I leaned over the boat's side as it was pulling away from the landing and bought two cans of soft drink. My change was getting further away from me very fast and I thought I could kiss it goodbye, when the vendor rolled the money into a ball and threw it at me. All those evenings playing cricket with the boys had not been wasted. I could still field a catch.

Susan was good company once I got over staring at her bald head. She told me that she had shaved it in a moment of weakness, thinking it would be less trouble when travelling. It might have been, but she had forgotten that she was heading north into a bitter winter and she was already feeling the cold.

We passed several of the ocean-going ships that navigate this river, countless hefty coal barges, and other large passenger riverboats like ours. One riverboat had a top deck that was covered by a roof with turned up corners and looked like a monstrous, multi-storied pagoda. Another looked like a tiered wedding cake. Towards sunset we pulled past one more big town, and after that the river traffic lessened somewhat.

By this time I was fed up with the nagging voice that harangued us continuously with political propaganda from a loudspeaker on the wall of our cabin. It started at the crack of dawn, when all good communists should be up and about, but this bad capitalist had no intention of being so rudely aroused. Getting out my nail scissors I performed a highly successful laryngectomy on The Voice.

Stretched across the ship's prow was a sitting/dining room that was reserved for the use of the second-class citizens. Meals were not served here, but it was a comfortable place to sit and look out at the river. In the sitting room I met a businessman from Taiwan, and Susan and I went to lunch with him. The food was stone cold and not very appetising and the dining room was a dingy dump. Functional and institutional, it had a metal floor and unpolished wooden tables and chairs.

In dramatic contrast, the second-class sitting room had no food but tables covered with white cloths and graced with plastic flowers, a sideboard full of cups and plates, lino tiles on the floor and an enamel po spittoon beside each armchair. I was fascinated by the overhead decorations. There was a large recessed square in the centre of the ceiling that contained white wooden panels embossed with dragons and two 1960s five-armed light pendants. And from all around the edges of the square purple plastic grapes dangled invitingly.

Not wanting to face the fare of the boat's dining room again, Susan and I had instant noodles, fruit and beer for dinner, all of which we had bought very cheaply on our forays ashore. The fruit – mandarins, pears and bananas – was especially good. That night I subdued the neighbours by banging my elbow on the wall and roaring, 'Quiet!' and, though we stopped several times to load and unload cargo, I slept well.

Early in the morning, we pulled into a large town, and I dashed ashore to buy breakfast: more pickled eggs, sticky rice wrapped in bamboo leaves, one of the popular, but obscenely red sausages and a big lidded enamel pannikin for hot drinks.

For quite a while now both riverbanks had been covered with trees and by midday kilometre after kilometre of bamboo waved in the wind. Behind it stood forests of poplar and pine and among the trees I glimpsed the odd red roof. Gradually a mountain range crept up, fold on fold, as a backdrop to the river. On a headland further on, I saw a pagoda on top of a towering rock at the river's edge. The Precious Stone Castle can be seen for many kilometres coming or going on the river and has been poised on this peak for 1500 years.

That evening Susan and I braved the boat's kitchen again. This time we tried the soup. Served in real soup-kitchen style – slopped with a bent tin ladle from a huge, battered aluminium can as big as an oil drum – it was a greyish conglomeration in which vegetables and dumplings floated. Despite its unalluring appeal, however, it tasted fine, and I was enjoying it until I came across a dead match. Susan laughed so much at this I told her I hoped she had the cigarette butt.

Various members of the boat staff had told me, in pantomime, that our ETA next morning was six, seven, eight, and nine o'clock. But we actually landed in Wuhan at ten. The day had dawned wet, cold, misty and drab. Visibility was nil and no town was in sight. The weather did not clear and we went ashore, up a long metal ramp, in a damp, steady drizzle. Later I saw that the river here was a mile wide, lined with hideous black factories and fronted by long, flat steps that looked like the ghats on the Ganges.

Wuhan, at the confluence of the Yangtze and Han rivers, was established in about 600 BC. Now one of China's largest cities, it is a key traffic junction as well as an industrial centre. The river here is vital but perilous; its banks are lined by high dykes that obscure it from the town, but which failed to save it from the last great flood in 1983. Foreign trading concessions were established in Wuhan in 1861 and it has many fine nineteenth-century buildings in the German municipal style. There is also a 400 year-old Gui Yuan temple that houses a white jade Burmese Buddha with a large diamond in its forehead. The tomb of the Marquis Yi, which was discovered in 1978, is close to Wuhan. The Marquis lived in the 5th century BC and died, greatly mourned, at the age of twenty-five. He was buried with his dog, twenty-one female sacrifices, enough treasure to stock several museums and a couple of orchestras worth of musical instruments.

Susan was leaving by train for Beijing that evening and I had to buy a ticket on a boat going the rest of the way to Chongqing. We entered the enormous boat terminal complex, which resembled a cross between a massive riverboat and the Sydney Opera House. After many false starts, I was taken in hand by a kind woman who led me through the offices, until we were behind a counter where a row of ladies sat dispensing tickets. This was a new angle for me – it felt like being backstage, behind the scenery. Wherever it was, I was promptly supplied with a ticket.

Susan and I then attempted to find a phone, so that she could contact the agent who held her train ticket. But in the entire terminal there was not one public phone. Once again we were taken in hand by helpful local people. This time a delightful young couple found the left luggage room for me and a public phone for Susan. The phone was in a booth on the street and was guarded by an attendant.

We crossed the road and entered an upmarket Chinese restaurant where we had a very poor meal of what was alleged to be pork and eggs. My plate came covered with something that looked like runny baked custard. Some of the prices on the restaurant's menu were astronomical, especially for exotic items like snake. Susan read to me, 'Steak and eggs, 480 yuan. That's a bit hot!' I replied, 'Put your glasses on, that's snake and egg'. And it was.

When we left it was still cold and raining. In the street we sloshed past some great Victorian buildings and entered the marvellous Bank of China. It had massive chandeliers, carved wooden Corinthian columns, wonderful leather couches and a polished dance floor between the tellers and the customers. Outside the bank, in stark contrast, a destitute old man in rags huddled under a pedestrian overpass trying to elude the rain.

Still hungry, we came upon a McMuck. At least there were no surprises on your plate there. Later we stood on a street corner looking lost. A Chinese man with good intentions, but no English, offered us help and so did a westerner, the first we had seen since Shanghai, who had lots of English, but turned out to be even more lost than we were.

Susan and I parted at the train station and I returned to the boat terminal over the long suspension bridge that crosses the river at Wuhan and joins the two halves of the city. Except for this great bridge and the elegant old buildings, Wuhan seemed a cheerless town. The gate of the gangway that led to the riverboat was defended by an ogress who demanded six yuan to unlock it. I thought this was an extortion racket, but it turned out to be an official fee. I was given a ticket that entitled me to enter the first-class waiting room where you could avoid the rabble in the comfort of deep lounge chairs. There were fees for everything you did in China, especially if you were a foreigner. I had even been charged five yuan to cross the bridge in the taxi.

My next ship, the *Jade Vessel*, was almost identical to the *Yangtze Star*. Once again I had an outside cabin, but this time the deck area beside my cabin was enclosed by glass windows. The attendant brought me five cakes of soap. I must have looked like I needed a good wash.

We glided away downriver in the silvery gloom of dusk. As we passed under the looming suspension bridge, it was almost dark and the town lights and those of nearby ships twinkled cheerily. My cabin companion this time was a diminutive Chinese girl of about twenty, who put her pyjamas on ready for bed at seven and still had them on at lunch the next day. I drew my bed curtains and read while she snored.

I slept snug and warm in my bed after I had shut up another lot of rowdies next door by elbow bangs on the wall. But I discovered that it was freezing cold and pitch dark out on the river when, in the middle of the night, I had to go down the deck to find the loo. Coming back I had a fearful time finding my door again and, palpitating and expecting to find myself in someone else's cabin, I opened what I hoped was the right one.

I was again woken at dawn by The Voice harassing me from the loudspeaker on the wall but, praise be! I found that this machine had a knob with which it could be turned off. To no avail, it turned out. The speakers in the cabins on either side were so loud that I could still hear it anyway. The Voice went on and on in a maddening shriek, probably exhorting me to be a good little worker and grow more rice. Then the cabin attendant barged in. There was no stopping her. She was programmed to sweep the floor at eight and that was what she did.

It was still very cold. As I watched the dismal grey rain drizzling down, I wondered why I had thought I was leaving this weather behind in Beijing. It was actually colder here. More doleful towns lined the riverbank and more grim chimneys belched smoke from dark forbidding factories. In one town a ferry, with a truck leaning precariously sideways on its slanting deck, was being pushed across the river by a tug. We gave it a couple of blasts on the hooter to get it out of the way. Just past the town a large solitary farmhouse owned a quiet stretch of riverbank. Steps led down from the house to its dunny, a box on stilts conveniently positioned over the water.

Although the traffic on the river had been lighter since Wuhan, a slow, steady procession of sampans and barges with loads of logs, sand, building materials and coal passed us. Sometimes three or four barges were joined together side by side and pushed upriver by a tug that was secured between them. The barges had two double-storeyed edifices roosting on their bows. One was the engine room, the other the cookhouse and bedroom. A particularly decrepit, unpainted and rusty old barge went by. The housewife (or bargewife) sat on deck on a wooden stool peeling vegetables. The husband came to the door of the cookhouse and threw his washing water overboard from a white enamel basin.

The river here was still at least two kilometres wide – I could see only one bank, which had greenery on it that looked like bamboo – but the water was flatter, there were no white caps, and it was the colour of dark milky tea. It did not agree with my hair and I sincerely hoped I was not drinking it. But I probably was: I had to use the hot water provided by the boat's urns for tea and noodles, and all our boat's refuse, like everyone else's, went straight into the river.

Later our boat tied up at a pontoon on the riverbank of Yeoyang. I ventured onto the shore to buy supplies of nuts, seeds, fruit and noodles. I thought the nuts and seeds were awful, until I saw someone else eating them and realised that you don't eat the outer husks. You spat them out in true Chinese fashion, preferably on the floor. This improved the taste considerably!

The next day was still cold and the sky was leaden and misty. The river was now the colour of dishwater – a pale ash-brown – the washing up after a mud pie party. When I woke, we were anchored at Shashi, another sombre industrial town. Shortly after Shashi the banks of the river came close enough for me to be able to see rice growing on them. In places the banks had been cut and reinforced with stones to form dykes. Another bank further up protected neat and pleasantly green villages that were surrounded by pine trees. Grazing cows dotted grassy banks where now and then I saw the odd peasant digging. These were the first real villages I had seen, as opposed to small ugly towns.

Although the *Jade Vessel* was very similar to the *Yangtze Star*, much to my sorrow there were no plastic grapes in the sitting room. But it did have two classes of dining room, the posher of which I fronted to sample the fare. In the long wait for my food to be sent up to the ritzy dining room, I watched a man drink a bottle of Chinese whisky and down a large bottle of beer as a chaser. When the food did arrive it turned out to be the same food that was available downstairs; not very good, just colder after its travels. I had chicken that had been machettied into clumps, splintery bones and all, but it was a change from the fruit and noodles I had been existing on.

Out on deck, nailed to the front of the wheel-house, I noticed the boat's emergency equipment – a big axe and a crowbar. The fire-fighting apparatus consisted of a row of red buckets that served only to decorate the prow; they held at most half a pail of old rusty water. There were no life boats or jackets – we swam or sank.

Gliding under a long bridge, we began passing between slight hills that rose on both sides of the now narrowing river. Gradually the hills increased in number and size until they were rounded mountain bosoms that rose straight up from a rocky base at the water's edge. The mountains were interspersed wherever possible with tiny rice terraces and here and there harboured a house. It was now freezing. Heaters and reverse cycle airconditioners abounded, but not one worked.

In the sitting room of the boat, I had company; four young men who played cards, a popular pastime, and smoked heavily, as did most Chinese men. Later the men played checkers, another favourite Chinese game.

Arriving at the large town of Zhicheng, we found an enterprising row of vendors had lined up on the edge of the pontoon and were conveying noodles, rice and drinks to customers on the boat by means of a basket on a long pole. The money came back down, with any luck, the same way. Other sellers paddled up on the river side of the boat in sampans and also sent goods aboard by the pole method.

The cook, wearing her red carpet slippers and still

knitting – Chinese women knitted everywhere, even standing up – went down onto the landing and had a social gathering with her family who had been waiting there for the boat to arrive. I defied the spitting rain to go ashore in search of food. The word must have been broadcast that culinary delights on riverboats were few and flawed. Passengers were offered plenty of edible supplements at all the stops we made, and a profusion of buyers eagerly contested them. I bought hard-boiled eggs and bread sticks that were plaited in a pretty design, but rock hard, and on which I broke a large tooth filling.

One day I looked at the sludgey mud pie that remained in the base of my empty thermos and concluded that by this time I must have taken in a fair slab of the Yangtze's bottom. But what a blessing those battered tin thermoses were. They provided water for instant noodles, tea, coffee, a wash, clean teeth and drinking water, as well as adding a bit of silt to the diet.

At each stop, crowds of passengers bustled on and off the boat. I noticed men holding pieces of bamboo loitering among the crowd. I wondered what this piece of equipment was for until I realised that it was the stock in trade of the porter coolie. This was the pole that he lay across his shoulders to carry burdens and bundles on each end.

Early the next day, we came to Yichang, a walled city that was new in the days of the Sui, about 1300 years ago, and which is regarded as the gateway to the upper Yangtze. The riverbank here was high and reinforced by a stone wall. On one corner of it there was a pagoda, and a promenade lined by trees ran along its top for kilometres.

We tied up at the town for an hour and then, moving into the middle of the river, dropped anchor with a rattle of chain. It was raining heavily and the boat's red-painted decks were washed clean and shining. We stayed anchored in mid-stream all day, left at five in the evening, and arrived at the entrance of the massive Gezhouba Dam's locks at night.

By the ship's searchlight, in the driving rain, I saw sheer concrete walls that rose, glistening, a hundred metres above me on both sides. It was like being in a grave. The lock was just wide enough to accommodate our boat. Seven ships, big and small, were tied to brackets in the walls, one behind the other. Then the gates were opened, the water poured in, and we were lifted slowly to the level of the road alongside the lock. As the boat rose, I went from only being able to see concrete walls, to seeing the lights of the town. Leaving the lock I looked down on the floodlit muddy water to see the salvo of polystyrene containers that our boat had left behind.

We were now about to enter the beautiful, but treacherous, Yangtze gorges. The Sanxia (Three Gorges) run for two hundred kilometres through the mountain ranges that separate the provinces of Sichuan and Hubei. They were created by an inland sea that once flooded across the Asian continent to the Pacific Ocean. For centuries the reefs and whirlpools of the gorges claimed a thousand lives a year. The forces of nature on the Yangtze are so great that many myths have grown up to help make sense of them. It is said that junk-men used to cut off a rooster's head and smear its blood on the prow of their boat to placate the river dragons. Fifty years ago boats were pulled through the gorges by thousands of straining coolies.

In our boat the helmsman's assistant stood at the very front of the prow, his eyes fixed ahead, and gave the captain signals. I could feel the tension. There is no room for error between the Yangtze gorges. We crept forward, our way lit by the boat's searchlight and the warning beacons that clung here and there on the dark rock edges between the wild water. It was magic.

At dawn I looked out to see that we had anchored in the

second gorge to wait for enough light to navigate further. The river here was too deadly to take on at night. The narrow walls of the gorge looked as though they had been cut out with a giant knife. A torrent of water rushed between their sheer rock faces that rose straight up as high as nine hundred metres and enclosed us on either side. We pushed on laboriously. It seemed difficult to make headway against the current. Every now and then the white thread of a small waterfall cascaded down to join the river. Narrow and fast flowing, they zig-zagged through dark-green slots in the black rock. A lone brown falcon cruised past, rising and falling effortlessly on the eddies that formed in the narrow chasm.

The river channel became even narrower and the boat had to dodge rocks that stuck up out of the water. As we struggled through one dangerous part, the water boiled towards us and tossed the boat around like a cork. Then the river widened and the channel was marked by buoys on boat-shaped platforms. The walls changed to yellow and white limestone and were dotted with mysterious-looking caves. Coffins containing bronze swords and other artefacts have been discovered in these caves. They are said to have belonged to an ancient tribe of the Warring States period – 500 BC – whose custom was to place their dead in these high mountains.

Our captain obviously understood the river. At times he steered well away from the water's edge where I discerned evil-looking whirlpools. But we passed some of them close enough to see several feet down into their swirling, seething, terrifying depths.

When we emerged from the gorges, everything was lightly veiled in early morning mist. The river was now a hundred metres across, but still boisterous, as it surged in front of the boat. Steep mountains folded one after the other into the churning brown water ahead, hiding the course of the river.

We passed several riverboats going down river. That voyage took three days as opposed to the five it needed to battle upriver against the enormous current, which probably explained why I was the only foreigner aboard.

The boat was now sailing very close to one bank where, on a steep cliff at a bend of the river, a monastery hung out over the water. Perched precariously, halfway up on the sheer rock face, it seemed to cling by its fingernails to the bare stone. The edges of its roof curled upwards like hands lifted to heaven. Perhaps it was built on this high, remote and beautiful spot to make the monks feel closer to God.

A fisherman wearing a traditional straw hat sat with a scoop net where the bank, which was still all steep rock, sloped a little to afford a toe hold. Close by, a tiny village surrounded by terraced gardens squatted halfway up a mountain. Partly obliterated by trees and shrubs, it looked ancient and inaccessible. Miles from anywhere, I wondered how you would get into it, or out, for that matter. I could see no roads. Behind the village the mountain peaks were even higher, and only great stretches of uncultivated and deserted mountains followed it.

(Sadly, much of this wild beauty is about to be inundated with water as the Sanxia Dam project progresses. Due for completion in the year 2009, this colossal enterprise will be the world's largest water reservoir. Located thirty-eight kilometres upstream from the present dam, it will cost twenty billion American dollars, provide electricity equal to one fifth of China's present generating capacity, control floods – the last flood in 1992 claimed over 200,000 lives – and make the river more easily navigable. It will also necessitate the relocation of more than 250,000 people from the area the lake will cover, submerge unexplored archaeological sites, most likely kill species not yet discovered and destroy the unique loveliness of the gorge area, which I was glad that I'd had the chance to see now.)

Then the land levelled a little and larger plots that were being ploughed by oxen or bullocks appeared, while goats, stark white against the dark green, clambered about on the precipitous hillsides. The villages comprised a series of tall thin buildings with mottled grey or yellow walls and tiled roofs. Some villages looked like fortresses.

Finally, I caught a glimpse of what, from the paintings I had seen and the poetry I had read, I had expected of China; terraces planted with gardens and crops that wound around the mountain slopes in soft green furrows like the lines on a child's top or a shih tzu dog's face, and among groves of pine trees and waving bamboo an occasional mellow village or house.

At Fengjie, the ancient capital of the state of Kui, six hundred stone steps led up from the water to a stone archway above the entrance of the town. Both sides of the steps were littered with shanties and shacks, but the town above had some fine buildings. We tied up at the pontoon wharf, and I went up on deck to lean on the railing. In an open-air waiting room on the pontoon, at eye level, fifty people sat entranced in front of a lone television set. One noticed me and shouted, 'Loala!' Fifty pairs of eyes at once swivelled from the magic of the screen to fix on me. I was much more riveting than the soap opera they had been watching.

Later that day we passed another large town. Sitting on ledges that had been cut into the top of the high bank, the town was surrounded by the black steps of an open-cut coal mine. Tall chimneys belched coal smoke over the grimy buildings in a dismal scene.

In sharp contrast, shortly after leaving this nightmare, a kaleidoscope of soft greens – vegetables, rice and bamboo – rose to carpet the sloping riverbanks until they met the luminous misty woods that stood above.

A mini magpie the size of a swallow had joined the boat.

He adopted the front deck as his home and chirped away as he patrolled it on foot. I'll bet he found a fair bit to eat there. The Chinese wasted an incredible amount of food on this boat as I had seen them do in many other places. In the dining room I watched a young mother and her tiny child eating. The baby would not have been more than two years old, but his diminutive fingers handled chopsticks deftly. He dipped and delved, picking up and transferring pieces of food from the communal plate to his bowl with a dexterity that made me envious. When he and his mother had finished their meal, more than half of the food they had ordered was left on the table.

Four hours later we arrived at Wanxian, the next big river settlement, and a town of some consequence. It had a grand clock tower, and hundreds of wide steps, like the Spanish steps in Rome, led up to it. The houses of the town, built on the second quarter of the sloping riverbank, looked like a pile of building blocks had been stacked up the rise. Hovels edged the low line of the river, sitting directly on the rock or silt. They were little more than bits of wood covered with sheets of plastic or tarpaulins and looked ready to be swept away with the next flood.

I hung over the deck railing looking down on the landing, watching coolies bent double with great weights offload stores from the lower cargo deck. A pretty young girl in the crowd glanced up and saw me. Her eyes widened and I saw her lips form the dreaded, 'Loala!' Her companions then stared up at me too. How I had come to hate that word!

On the outskirts of Wanxian we passed many gaunt buildings that rose from the riverbank as though they had grown out of its grey mud. Among them an enormous chimney billowed forth a massive cloud of sulphur smoke which the wind snaked along the mountains, the town and the valley like a scarf that half veiled them. When I looked back from kilometres further up the river, I could still see the smoke hanging low and partly obscuring the view.

As evening approached, the river became wilder and we moved into ever higher and denser mountains. Great towering monsters that soared, peak after peak, line after line, all around and formed a dark blue backdrop for the gathering grey mist. When night fell, we were gliding – the throbbing engines pushing us slowly against the rushing water – into the deepening gloom and the mountains that appeared to sink into the water ahead. I felt as though we were being swallowed up.

During the night, we crawled along, at times very close to the banks, as the captain, aided by his spotlight, felt his way between the green pinpoints of light from the beacons. I could see, high above, the towering tops of the mountains dimly outlined against the velvet night sky. Now and then their sides were dotted by a small yellow glow from a house or the cluster of lights of a village sparkling in the warmish night. We had turned south again. And among the gorges, or folded in the arms of the mountains as we were now, it was not as cold as when we had been exposed out on the open river.

My cabin mate had got off the boat at Wanxian and it was a pleasure to sleep alone for the first time in over a week. Next morning, in desperation, I had a cold shower. There was only hot water in the evening, but usually at a time when the bathroom had already been locked for the night to protect it from violation by the lower orders. I hung my washing on the rail outside my door where it flapped merrily, drying in the breeze. The other passengers, also inspired by the warm air, indulged in an orgy of cleanliness and all along the deck, trousers, shirts and undies fluttered in gay abandon.

At five that evening we approached Chongqing, a city with a 3000-year-old history. In the Qin dynasty of the third century BC, it was the capital of the kingdom of Ba. Following the Japanese invasion in the second world war, it became the capital of Chiang Kai-shek's Kuomintang and was heavily bombed. Built on the mountain-sides of a promontory between the confluence of the Yangtze and the Jialing rivers, it is the major city of Sichuan province and is crucial to transport and commerce. But approaching Chongqing I could hardly see it for the great clouds of smoke that belched from the factory chimneys.

Our boat tied up alongside another, which we had to climb over to reach the landing. I could manage my two bags fairly easily by myself, but as soon as I stepped off the boat I was mobbed by a pack of would-be porters who swarmed around me like angry bees. I can cope with being harassed and accosted, but this gang of vultures grabbed the bags out of my hands and knocked me about in the process. None of the Chinese passengers got this treatment. I resisted and standing my ground, tore my bags back. 'No!' I said vehemently. But they followed me, yelling in my ears. I made it across the boat, down the gangplank and onto the landing unaided, but the porters continued to pester me. At the bottom of the gangplank, I stood behind the guard, who got the message and chased my assailants off. But they only went a certain distance, like jackals from a kill. I said thank you to the guard very politely, which, to my horror, inspired him to grab one particularly persistent coolie and give him a hiding. No one took any notice. But it bothered me.

On the other side of the landing I was confronted by a flight of stone steps that went up to the sky. My jaw dropped and I thought, No way! I'm not climbing five hundred steps carrying these bags. I turned to a young coolie who, unlike the others, had not been aggressive but had just stood back and offered me a price. 'Okay mate, it's all yours,' I said. He took the bags, I put my mountaineering legs into gear, and up we went.

The steep stone steps did not appear to have been cleaned since the Ming dynasty. They were overlaid with mud which made the ascent hazardous and mucky. At the top of the first flight the porters re-appeared. They had given up on carrying my bags and, now, having decided I wouldn't make it the rest of the way, wanted to carry me. The final indignity! When I declined their chair lift, the porters wanted to hold me under the arms and support me. I shooed them off and made it to the top only to encounter another gang of sharks – rip-off taxi drivers quoting ridiculous prices. Knowing that the hotel I wanted was close, I took out my guidebook to show one driver where I wanted to go. A crowd of hundreds instantly materialised and leaned over me to peer at the book. I was squashed in the middle of this mob and developing a galloping case of claustrophobia when I saw my saviour drive up, a young woman in a miniature taxi. I grabbed her and jumped in her car.

4 Three Dog Night

The taxi driver seemed to understand where I wanted to go. I squeezed myself and my bags into her micro-dot vehicle and off we rattled. At the hotel the notorious discrimination against 'big noses' was blatantly exposed in writing. A large sign on the wall listed two prices, Chinese and Foreigner, and the latter was three times the former! I complained, but the price did not come down.

I sought fresh fields. The next hotel recommended in my book, the Huixianlou, had the same nefarious sign displayed at the reception desk and Foreigners' rooms were again grossly over-priced. On principle I refused to subscribe to this highway robbery. I was not going to pay such a fee for a room that I knew would not necessarily be clean and most certainly would not have all its accoutrements working. For that price in other countries I could get a positively sanitary hotel room where everything worked, at least someone spoke my language and I was not ill-treated, disdained and ridiculed. The receptionist offered me an eight-bed dormitory for ten dollars. I took it.

The room actually had seven beds. Either the staff couldn't count, or the rats ate the other one – there were enough of them, rats that is, not beds. And they had company. The hotel was also infested with cockroaches.

The beds were crammed together in the room, but only one appeared to be occupied. When I returned late that night, I found, to my astonishment, that the owner of the other bed was a young Japanese man. I had presumed that communal rooms would be segregated. Sharing a hotel room with a strange young man was a bit of a novelty, but no problem. Hiro was amiable and easy to get on with, despite the fact that he had three words of English and I only knew two of Japanese. I gave him some pills and bananas to settle his crook tummy and after two days he was better and we parted good friends. Co-habiting was, in fact, amusing. One morning we wanted hot water to make tea. I said, 'I'll get it.' Hiro said, No, he would. We came out of our room together, he clutching the water jug and I, holding the thermos. A pile of Chinese who were waiting for the lift goggled. A Chinese man – and my Japanese friend could have passed for one – getting off with a foreign woman, is punishable practically by death in this country. I had read horror stories about western men ending up in gaol just for being seen with a Chinese girl.

The dormitory was on the ninth floor and had extensive windows that gave a good view, but also vertigo. The impression I got was that Chongqing was made up of building construction sites. Wherever I looked, cranes pierced the sky and a constant racket of pile drivers and bulldozers hammered at my eardrums. A great empty pit yawned directly below me and from it to the end of the street everything had been demolished. The only intact structures I could see were the produce markets that were housed in what looked like heritage railway sheds two streets away.

The Hotel Huixianlou was in the process of being remodelled, which meant that its prices would go up. In my room, half the light bulbs were blown, cold air poured in through big gaps where the windows didn't fit adequately, the wall paper was peeling off in strips, the cases of the airconditioners – which of course didn't work – were missing and two of the wall lights hung from their fittings by a thread. The room had a television with no sound and one cupboard, padlocked shut! The beds had no mattresses. You slept on one blanket spread on a flat wooden base. A tiny pillow and one more blanket (they were rationed one to a bed) made up the sleeping apparatus. I pillaged more blankets from the spare beds. It was still fairly cold. I had hoped that this far south the weather might be warmer – but Chongqing is high in the mountains.

Wondering why I could hear the guests in the adjoining room so clearly, and smell their cigarette smoke, I discovered that the walls at both ends of my room were only thin partitions. My bed was against one of these and a gap gave me, if I had been so inclined, direct access to my neighbours. Lovely people, they came home at two or three in the morning, shouting and screaming and blew cigarette smoke in my face as I lay in bed.

As soon as I had staked my claim to a piece of the dormitory, I went for a walk. The Hotel Huixianlou is in one of Chongqing's main streets that are lined with shops. They were mostly small places that sold clothing, but there were a couple of big department stores. In all the shops the merchandise – even torch batteries and chewing gum – was safely locked away under glass. Then, as an added safeguard, a sentinel was stationed at the exit. Even a posh furniture shop came complete with a guard at the door – to stop you walking in, picking up a sofa and making off with it under your jacket.

Near the hotel I found a very lively night market. Although it was quite dark by then, I felt safe wandering around it, until I became aware that two young blokes were following me and eyeing my handbag. I slowed up and meandered along, stopping now and then until they had to pass me. Then I followed them. They kept looking around to see where I was, but it's hard to mug someone who is in the crowd behind you.

I went into a restaurant and with the help of the phrasebook asked what their specialty was. The waitress pointed to an item at the top of the Chinese only menu. I said, 'Okay.' A big heap of chunky chopped meat, cauliflower, eggs and gravy was conjured up. I had no idea what it was, but later I read that the specialty of this area was dog. And when I saw skinned dog carcases, all red and bloody, but identifiable because the heads had been left on, hanging in the market, I knew that what I had enjoyed was man's best friend, Fido. A restaurant I frequented later sported a glass-fronted charcoal grill in which three dogs complete with heads and crisp brown barbecued skin rotated.

I did not get much sleep that night. The building construction continued, under floodlights, beneath and all around me. Bulldozers, cranes, jack-hammers and pile drivers roared, thumped and bumped, accompanied by whistle blasts and yells until after one a.m. Then very early in the morning the clamour started again. When the building noise stopped my rowdy neighbours took over, rested briefly, then started up again at five to compete with the construction teams. This went on every night I spent in Chongqing, but I survived by using ear-plugs.

For all that, I decided that I liked Chongqing. Its streets were narrow, bent and twisty and went up and down crazily, but there were no bicycles. This was not bicycle country; men did all the packwork. Everywhere I looked I saw coolies in ragged blue Mao jackets walking about with their poles and ropes hoping for some chance employment, or bearing the most incredible loads on their shoulders.

In the morning the bathroom taps produced no hot water, so I set off largely unwashed to find the Public Security Bureau (the police). My visa was about to expire and the PSB were reputed to supply extensions, albeit for a substantial fee. I asked the hotel receptionist to write down the address of PSB and astounded myself by finding it easily. After walking a little way, I had gone into a shop to ask directions. A young girl took me by the hand, led me next door to the PSB office and sat me down. The visa was accomplished reasonably painlessly in about an hour at a cost of ninety-five yuan and was presented to me by a beautiful young lady dressed in police uniform, plain navy slacks, jumper and shoes. With no embellishments or a single drop of make up, she was still stunning.

Another young woman sat on the bench beside me and helped me fill out my form. She told me that she was getting an exit visa for her boss who needed to travel on business. An attractive young man took my application then sat at his desk reading the paper and extensively and diligently picking his nose. What an excavation job he did, first with one hand, then the other, to make sure he got it all. He rolled up what he found and dropped the end product on the floor. When he had completed this routine to his satisfaction, he started on his ears. Unfortunately I had to leave before I could see what came next.

Much elated at achieving an extension of stay without the problems I had heard could be attached to it, I started my next mission – to buy a ticket onwards. Having read that it was possible to travel further on the river by smaller boat and that the Chongqing Hotel had a travel department, I went there and tried to extract some information. But the travel agent was only programmed to sell tickets on a tourist boat that did short river trips. She knew of nothing that was available elsewhere, not even in the next town. But the young man at reception produced a map and showed me that it was possible to go to Wuhan.

I said, 'I have just come from there. I want to go the other way, to Leshan, or another place further along the Yangtze.'

'Not possible,' he replied.

I argued that it was and showed him my guidebook. Beaten into submission he said, 'Okay. Yes you can go to Leshan.'

Suddenly, he knew all about it. 'But,' he said, 'it's no good boat. You not like it. Why not fly?'

End of story. There was no way I would fly in China. I also decided against Leshan. The boat's timetable was unreliable and irregular. Going to Leshan also meant heading north again, and I was sick of being cold. I wanted to go south, so I decided on a train to Guangzhou.

It was now lunchtime and, as the guidebook said that good food was to be had at the Chongqing Hotel, I tried their restaurant. The menu had an English translation and attempts at western dishes, but the specialty listed was dog. I ordered rabbit, hoping that wasn't an euphemism for rat, which were plentiful in Chongqing. Apart from the battalion that shared my room with me, I saw several well-fed rats lying dead in the gutters. The meat I ate was hot and spicy and, whatever it was, it tasted good, despite its having been chopped up brutally with a cleaver. Deciding to be utterly, decadently European, I ordered a banana split, but it was made from frozen milk with a couple of bits of banana thrown in. That's it, I concluded. I am done with Chinese versions of western food.

I took a taxi to the Remnin Hotel. A replica of Beijing's Temple of Heaven, a stupendous round edifice with a domed roof, in its former life it had been a palace. I went inside for a sticky-beak and while there I decided to look up CITS which the book said was at this address. Despite a huge sign on the outside wall of an adjoining building that declared CITS to be lurking within, this involved much difficulty. I could not locate an entrance. I walked all around the wall and back again, but still found no doorway. Finally, I went up some stairs on one side and found some doors – all with indecipherable Chinese signs. One of the doors was open, so I knocked and entered. A young man was stretched out asleep on a couch. In due time he made me very welcome and did not seem upset that I had disturbed his nap. But the young man couldn't understand me, and he had to send for re-enforcements. Eventually five men were in the room, smoking, reading the paper, or interrogating me. They could tell me nothing about onward travel. One young man spoke fairly good English. He said he listened to Radio Australia every morning. He tried to help me, but right or wrong he wanted to put me on a plane. I said. 'I don't want to go on a plane.' He was amazed. 'You don't like to fly with CAAC!'

'Listen, mate', I said. 'I like to live, that is why I don't like to fly with CAAC.'

He thought that was hilarious, but he still wanted to put me on a plane. I said, 'I want to go down to Guangzhou by train.' At first he denied that there was any such creature, but when I insisted there was, he gave in and admitted it. 'Yes, yes, yes. There is a train, but very awful and impossible to get a soft sleeper without waiting a very long time.'

'I don't mind', I said, 'I'll wait.'

He repeated that it was impossible.

I asked if he would phone the station to ask. That seemed terribly hard.

Finally he said, 'You wait. You wait.'

Fifteen minutes later another man was produced to make the phone call. After a long conversation, the first young man turned to me, 'You give me your passport and 1000 yuan for the train ticket.'

'A thousand!'

'Only yuan, not dollars.'

But a thousand was a bit hot. It cost only 600 yuan from Shanghai to Beijing and that was much further. I began to think that there was something peculiar going on here, so I tried to exit gracefully and make a fast getaway. This was not easy. And later, when I found out how much money these gents had lost because I would not cough up my cash, I understood why.

The soft sleeper on the next day's train to Guangzhou

would have cost me 360 yuan! How curious! In the event, I changed my mind and went to Liuzhou and Yanshu instead.

I walked around to view the Renmin Hotel from the front. It was spectacular. I attempted to climb a colossal flight of steps on one side of it but was stopped by a young woman who removed two yuan from me. I did not know why until I reached the top and discovered to my amazement that I had paid to watch a lecture on Chinese massage in a monstrous auditorium. The inside of the auditorium was as magnificent as the original Temple of Heaven. I gawked and came down again. A pleasant garden at the bottom of the steps led to the street from where I took a taxi to the railway station.

At the station I encountered massive problems just finding the ticket offices, let alone the one that sold tickets to Guangzhou. Pointing to 'I want to buy a ticket' in my book, I wandered around an immense area asking one person after another until I finally came to the right place. There I was confronted by row after row of counters with little windows that had Chinese writing above, and long queues in front of them. I continued asking and was directed to one. But after standing in line for ages, I decided that the prices listed above the window could not be enough to get me to Guangzhou. I moved in front of a window with large prices and the shortest waiting line and when I reached the counter I pointed to Guangzhou in my book. It did not surprise me when the ticket seller said that I was at the wrong window. She pointed to where I should be.

What did surprise me was to see people standing patiently in queues. They were better behaved than their northern cousins – possibly because they had to stand between two lines of strong iron bars that they could not get over. But they could go past on one side. I saw one man walk along this side of the queue, shove his money in the window in front of the first person in line and buy a ticket. No grumbles were heard. No one complained. They just let him get away with it.

I got my message across to the ticket seller, a helpful woman who indicated that a soft sleeper to Guangzhou was not available for tomorrow. I asked if there was one to Liuzhou, which is close. She replied that there was. Only later, when I asked the hotel desk staff to translate my ticket for me, did I discover to my utter disgust that the train left at five o'clock in the morning! I had to clutch the desk to sustain the shock when this horror was revealed to me. It meant I had to get up in the freezing cold at three a.m.

Outside the station, a line of taxi vultures lurked. One grabbed me and pushed, patted and propelled me into his taxi. Then he demanded fifty yuan. I yelped, 'Not on your Nelly!' It had only cost nine to come there. I got out, slammed the door and walked off. He ran after me saying, 'Forty, thirty, twenty!' To which I genteely replied, 'Frogs!' Across the road I flagged a passing taxi with a working meter, who returned me for the price I had paid to get there.

After Hiro left, I had no company in my room, well not human anyway. As I was drawing the curtains at the far end of the room, I saw a furry thing moving on the floor. On closer inspection it proved to be a large rat in the process of twitching its death throes. Death from over-eating, by the look of it. I summoned the room maid, who very casually and calmly swept the rat up with her feather duster and put it in the bin. It looked like she did it all the time. During the night one of the deceased's brethren came looking for it. I was almost asleep when I felt a large animal jump on top of me and start walking down my hip. I gave a shriek and the rat went flying off. Next morning there was another very dead rat on the floor. I wondered if it was my nocturnal visitor who had died of a heart attack. I have been told that I have a scream like an air-raid siren.

At dusk that evening I went strolling along the streets

looking at the shops. It was a good time to be out; many people were shopping and temporary stalls, pedlars and night markets were active. Small boy shoe-shine merchants and a street ironer worked away on the footpath close to where an old woman in charge of a pair of bathroom scales invited custom. I saw a youth trying to sell the same armful of neck ties that I had seen him with in the morning and again at noon. He stood in front of a haberdashery shop that also sold ties. The tolerance of the shop keepers amazed me. They allowed hawkers to sell the same goods as they did, probably cheaper, right outside their doors.

The shops did not diversify in the goods they stocked; one tiny shop was full of umbrellas and another of hats. Some things were so cheap that I wished I had the baggage space to bring them home, like several pretty hats that were only two or three dollars each.

I wandered a long way up and down these fascinating narrow streets. When I decided to return, it was dark and I could not see anything familiar. Then I realised that I did not have the address of my hotel with me. I had no idea where I lived. I was lost, and I couldn't speak a word of the language. I had used a monument at an intersection near my hotel as a landmark, but when I returned to it in the dark it looked different and I had gone off in the wrong direction. I walked for a very long time before I came to a big hotel and, in desperation, I decided to swallow my pride and ask for aid.

It did not help that I could neither pronounce nor write my hotel's name and, although it turned out to be only three blocks away, the reception staff did not know the other hotels in their vicinity. Nevertheless the two male hotel staff were helpful. They pored over my map and eventually worked out that I had gone wrong at the monument. Thanking them profusely, I went back to it, found where I had made the mistake and was saved from a night on the streets.

The next morning I set off to get the filling I had lost on the boat replaced. I pantomimed 'sore tooth' to the hotel receptionist and she wrote the name of the hospital where I should seek help. It was not far and I walked, asking directions. I would not have known the building was a hospital if it had not been pointed out to me. There was an armed guard at the gate.

In the grounds I showed my paper to several people and was sent all over the place until a girl in a white uniform marched me to the dentistry department. My guide led me into the building, jumped the queue at the office where patients were waiting to register and, in exchange for the princely sum of eight cents, handed me a ticket that entitled me to treatment. The dental unit was, as usual for anything I wanted, up ten flights of stairs. I consoled myself with the thought that if there had been a lift, it would not have been working.

While I was hiking up all those steps I had plenty of time to think about chickening out. I had always dreaded the thought of being a patient in a Third World hospital and had sworn blind that no matter what happened to me I would never allow it. Before leaving home I'd had my teeth checked. The tooth that had lost its filling in the middle of a five-day jaunt on the Yangtze River had been the only one that had needed repairs. That dentist would be in a lot of trouble.

Before committing myself to the ministrations of a Chinese dentist, I carefully considered the pros and cons of the exercise. If I did not have the tooth treated, the worst thing that could happen was that I could lose it and suffer a lot of pain into the bargain. But if I had it filled I risked getting infected with HIV. The minute I set eyes on the building that housed the dental department I very nearly turned tail and bolted. Passing nurses and doctors in grubby white uniforms, I was led through alleys, grimy corridors and chilling waiting areas. Finally, I was put into a very large room that contained six dental chairs over which six dentists laboured.

Despite my fears, the dentists in their white coats looked reasonably clean. (The only really white coats I saw in China had been in a bank; for some obscure reason everyone in the place wore a coat of dazzling cleanliness.) A young dentist intimated that I should wait. There was not an enormous crowd of potential customers, the only place in China there wasn't.

In the fullness of time I was seated in the operating chair. The dentist and I indulged in some mutual pantomime. She seemed to be telling me what grisly procedure was necessary. All the other patients had brought along a couple of their relatives for moral support, but the next of kin, fickle things, immediately left their family member to the mercies of the ministering dentist so that they could attend the much more interesting spectacle of the foreign devil's exposed oral cavity. They flocked around the back of my chair, hustling for the best view. A few waiting patients joined the sideshow. They seemed to be telling the dentist to get on with it, 'If you are not treating this bloody foreigner why don't you let us in the chair? She's just hanging about doing nothing.' But we fought them off. One woman, whom I came to think of as the Inspector, took it upon herself to have a good look in my mouth every time the dentist did. Then she relayed what she'd seen to those behind, adding what was obviously either approval or disapprobation. I lay back in the chair under the spotlight, defeated.

Eventually a second opinion was brought in; an engaging young man, who spoke a few words of English, examined my mouth and said that he would have to repair the tooth and replace the filling. He had a wonderfully gentle touch that told me he knew what he was doing. I said, 'Go for it, son.' He produced a drill, something I regard as one of the more fiendish and macabre instruments of torture at the best of times, but this machine was decidedly elderly.

I think my dentist washed his hands, but he did not wear gloves and the same instruments and drill bits were used on everyone. They were only given a bit of a wipe with Metho. Enough to kill the AIDS and hepatitis viruses, I prayed.

Each dentist's chair was accompanied by a stand that had the operator's pieces laid out on it. My stand had a white top that was stained and far from clean. The torture implements lay in old chipped enamel bowls and the drill – Oooh the drill! And without an injection of local anaesthetic! Never in my worst nightmares had I ever imagined letting a dentist loose on me with a drill without an anaesthetic. I am a devout, card carrying, professed and practising coward. But there was no way I was going to have an injection in China. Among the emergency equipment I never travel without was a disposable syringe and needle, but the local anaesthetic sat on the shelf before me in multi-use quart bottles that were goodness knows how contaminated, so the syringe stayed in my bag. The fact that the drill might pierce my gum was enough to worry about. The dentist wiped the pointy bit with something on a swab which may have been disinfectant, but it could have been poison, for all I knew.

The performance began. Every cell in my body tensed, anticipating a slip of the instrument, as I dwelt on the knowledge that you only need a tiny unseen opening in your skin or mucosa to get infected. This gratifying thought did not make my stay in the chair a jolly or restful one, but it was certainly memorable. To take my mind off proceedings, I examined the window and the wall in front of me and concluded that the building had been hastily thrown together with a knife and fork. Everything was rough. The window ledge was crudely plastered, the window had been fitted crookedly and its wooden frame had had paint slopped over it haphazardly.

The operation on my tooth took a very long time. The dentist was elaborately painstaking and he did not have a nurse to help him. But even when he used the drill, this marvellous man was so gentle that he only gave me a couple of stabs of pain. Finally he took a piece of glass, swiped it clean with a swab, mixed the filling and very carefully packed it into my tooth.

By this time the dentist and I had become the best of friends. I was full of gratitude and admiration for his skill, and my tooth was feeling better than it had for a long time. Then, deserting his post, the dentist personally escorted me back downstairs. He led me into the registry office where I was hit a further fee, the special foreigner's price of 300 yuan – fifty Australian dollars. When the four girls in the office saw the account that the dentist had made out they fell about laughing hysterically. I was sure that this was because it was for such an enormous amount of money. The Chinese only pay one yuan for everything.

The bad news was that I was told not to eat for the rest of the day and to add insult to injury, on reaching my hotel I had to walk up nine flights of stairs to get to my room to recover. The lift was not working because the electricity was off. The light, power and hot water went off regularly in Chongqing and it often stayed so for hours at a time. Sometimes when I was walking around the streets or the market at night, all the lights would suddenly go out. A loud, 'Oooh!' would go up from the crowd, but kerosene lanterns and torches would be quickly produced and, unperturbed, it would be business as usual.

Another companion moved in to share my room with me. Strangely, I knew him. It was Joe, the Englishman Susan and I had met in Wuhan. Joe had been travelling in China for several months, and he told me some of his interesting experiences as he bounced around the room trying all of the beds like a middle-aged, bearded Goldilocks. It beat me why – all the beds were identical. I worried that I would disturb Joe the next morning when I got up long before dawn to catch my train, but he was more concerned about the presence of rats.

I went looking for the thousand-year-old Luohan Temple – and found it! *Luohan* is a Buddhist term for the Sanskrit *arhat* – people who have released themselves from the bondage of greed, hate and delusion and obtained the status of saints or holy men. You entered the temple by turning off one of Chongqing's main streets and climbing up a very steep, skinny alley to a narrow gate. From there you took the steps up a further incline, and marvelled at the rock carvings and shrines set into the natural rock face. Old ladies tended the shrines, bringing the idols offerings of incense and flowers.

The Luohan complex contained several temples, the dwellings of the resident monks and the monastery. At its peak the temple had seventy monks, but now there are only about eighteen. In the grounds much fragrant incense was burning and candles, some of them gigantic, were being sold. In one place, luckily outside and away from the buildings, a great row of enormous red candles, enough to start a grand conflagration, roared and blazed away.

In one temple a colossal gold Buddha enclosed in a glass case beamed down on me. The main temple was home to five hundred life-sized painted terracotta statues of *arhats*. Row after row of them gazed down on you from where they sat on platforms a metre off the ground. The route around the statues was cordoned off with string, so that once you started you had to keep going until you came to the end and not miss any – unless you hopped under the string and then you would be lost. The place was a maze. Without the string, you would never have got out again. Round and round I went in the temple's dim recesses. Now and then I came across a big gold-plated Buddha or an attendant, old women or men murmuring low over their prayerbooks or reciting their beads. The statues were so uncannily life-like that it was spooky. I swore that at least one of them was alive. And every one was different. They were of all races and skin colours. The expressions on their faces all differed too; some were holy and saintly, some cheeky, some naughty, friendly or fun loving. Each *arhat*'s name was inscribed beneath his chair and each one held something, either a musical instrument, a child, an icon or an animal. Walking among them in the dark, gloomy atmosphere was a curious experience and when I came out of the temple it took a while to accustom myself to the light and the real world again.

My friend, Denise, an American Buddhist I had met on the Trans Siberian Express on my way to Mongolia, had told me that she thought the communists had only re-opened the monasteries in China as a source of loot from tourists, but I think some older people had kept their religion, albeit underground.

Chongqing also boasted other attractions. The United States and Chiang Kai-shek Criminal Acts Exhibition Hall was one. This offered such dubious enticements as a visit to the prison cells and torture chambers. No thanks. The dental department had been enough for me.

5 Snakes Alive!

At four in the morning I found a driver asleep in his taxi in front of the hotel. I poked him awake – drivers here weren't protected by the plastic shields that I had seen in taxis in Shanghai.

Off we drove through the pre-dawn mist. Suddenly I knew why a feeling of *de ja vu* had been haunting me since I had arrived in Chongqing. Seeing the city in the misty half light made the penny drop. It reminded me of Naples. It was nowhere near as beautiful, but the way the town ran clinging to the mountain-side along a cliff, and its narrow, crooked streets that went up and down all higgledy piggledy gave it a sense of familiarity. The memory of the two happy years I had spent in Naples will always remain with me.

Deposited at the train station entrance – I'd had to pay five yuan at the gate for the taxi to drive the extra hundred yards from the road to the building – I enquired after my platform and was shown five fingers twice, which I took to mean ten. Continuing on, I enquired twice more and got two more answers. One man pointed upstairs, but I could see there was no platform up there and another passenger told me that it was the one I was standing on, number five. I settled for that.

I stood waiting in the pool of harsh light that isolated the platform from the surrounding darkness, my breath steaming in the freezing air, and hoped I was in the right place. The train choofed in on time and to my relief it was the one I wanted. I settled into my soft sleeper compartment for a fourteen-hour ride; we were due to reach Liuzhou at seven the next morning. I had decided to go there and take a bus to Yanshu, where the country-side was said to be fascinating, and from where it was possible to travel to Guangzhou by road or river.

Departing Chongqing, we travelled among gigantic peaked mountains, part of the great ranges that run east and west across China and separate the agricultural areas. It was still dark. High up here daylight did not appear until after seven. Now and then the train passed small huts that were softly lit by kerosene lamps or candles and it was a strange feeling to look into their interiors as we rode by, like seeing flashes of a different world flicked on a screen.

The train went through the mountains via tunnels that followed one after the other, some stretching for kilometres. What an engineering feat the building of this railway had been! Considering that the country's first railway had only been commenced at Shanghai in 1875 and that it had proceeded merely a short distance before being torn up by angry, superstitious mobs, China had come a long way.

Initially the mountains were just wilderness, but later their steep sides were terraced to an incredible height. Rice and vegetables grew in tiny plots only a couple of feet wide. This was a green but stony province. The rugged cottages and houses in the villages we passed were all made of stone, as were the terrace walls that surrounded the small amount of land that was suitable for planting.

I went to the train's dining car to investigate the possibility of fodder. This was quite an occasion. I am not often up for breakfast at the hour that the Chinese indulge in it. I noticed that other hopeful feeders had tickets in front of them on their tables, and approached a small squat lady who, strategically positioned at the dining car entrance, seemed to be the source of the tickets. In exchange for five yuan a piece of paper was issued to me that in due time metamorphosed into a bowl of gruel and some dumplings – neither of which had any taste at all. Showing the small squat one the food list in my book, I did an Oliver Twist and asked for more. At first she said, 'No,' but then she relented and pointed to fried rice and egg. I was delighted. Fifteen minutes later I was happily wading through an egg chopped up on rice and a bowl of spicy soup with bits of tomato floating in it.

Then I fell on my bunk and slept like the dead for three hours. It was the best sleep I'd had for days. After that it was time to put the nose-bag on again. Lunch boxes were brought along on a trolley. For a small fee I was given two boxes, one containing plain rice, the other mangled bits of duck and lots of cabbage. I know the latter was fresh as I had seen enormous baskets of cabbages being brought aboard the train and lined up in the corridor outside the cook house.

At first I shared my compartment with only one gent, but in the evening two others joined us. My companion and I, who did not exchange one word after our initial 'Neehow' – I speak excellent Chinese, only one word, but it's perfect – consumed our lunch. Apart from his slurps and burps, and the noise of our neighbours in the next compartment chomping their food, we ate in silence.

By afternoon the train tracks were still running high along the sides of steep mountains. Looking down with an eagle eye I saw a pretty mosaic of villages and fields. White ducks paddled among flooded rice paddies. Tough-looking ponies carried goods in woven pannier baskets that hung on their sides, and peasants in pyjama suits hauled buckets or baskets on wooden yokes across their shoulders. Washing was spread out to dry on rocks beside one cottage where two children played, possibly both in the same family. Where were the Baby Police? You never saw two children together in the towns. Pine trees lined the slopes and by the side of the railway line flourished cascading plants with red berries like cottoneaster and creepers with white and yellow flowers. A boy riding a buffalo waved to the train from among foliage and bamboo that was so lush it brushed the carriages as we went past.

More mountains and tunnels followed as we passed downhill through smartly painted railway stations. I saw a military post by the side of the tracks; a small white-washed stone building that was guarded by a soldier with a rifle slung over his shoulder. I wondered what he was guarding and from whom.

Lower down the land became flatter and I saw oxen and buffalo pulling ploughs in some of the larger fields. All possible space had been planted. Beans grew at the edges of paddy plots and spinach and greens on the sides of roads. In some places the harvest had been completed and the new green shoots of a fresh rice crop were coming up. In the fields hay was stored in stooks that were shaped like witch's brooms or in small, round haystacks with peaked roofs that looked like goblin's houses.

The old ways continued here. I saw peasants harvesting in pre-revolution attire: a knee-length tunic girdled with a sash, loose mid-calf trousers and a round skull-cap for men, a three-cornered scarf for women. And some of the machines had been the latest model in the first century AD. I saw donkey-powered treadmills pumping water into canals and threshing machines that were operated by a person jumping up and down on a pedal.

At dinner time I gave the menu's promised 'pried snall in bear sauce' a miss, but the spicy Sichuan style cuisine was very good.

At one stage I was in the loo when the train stopped. There was a knock on the door, then a male guard barged in, ejected me and locked me out. Happily I hadn't been in mid-stream! The guards performed this routine at each station. I guessed that passengers were not trusted to refrain from using the toilet while the train was in the station. I watched the guard wash his hands and then dry them on the lace curtains of the corridor windows. It was not the first time I had seen this. I figured it must be common practice.

By eight in the evening I had three room-mates and they were all fast asleep. One snored loudly. Only one, I reflected. Must be my lucky day. I decided to take the hint and retire up to my bunk. I was reading Brendon Behan's, *Borstal Boy*, amazed to find that he'd had a better time in prison than I'd had in Saudi Arabia. There was not a lot of difference in the two lifestyles.

The night was long. The train was not terminating at Liuzhou and I worried that I might sleep through my stop. Finally I slept so well that I woke myself up snoring. I hoped I hadn't caught that from my neighbours – I might be spitting next. I had come to hate the sound of spitting. Even above the sound of the train I could hear people letting loose on the carpeted corridor outside my door.

When dawn came we were in wonderful country. Outside the window soared huge mountains decorated with patterns of limestone rock, green grass and wreathing fog. The sun came up, slanting between mist-shrouded groves of pine and bamboo. In the villages ducks, buffalo and peasants stirred for the day.

There were no more tunnels. Now we ran through deep cuttings between the mountains, or along their sides. Far away below a clear green river flowed. Nothing broke the mirror of the river's calm surface except a lone fisherman who rowed a small boat standing up. What a contrast to the fast, muddy Yangtze.

When I saw bananas growing my spirits lifted at this sign of a warmer climate. Further on flat fields of rice and vegetables stretched out to the horizon. A couple of large towns and more and more fields of food brought us finally to the city of Liuzhou in Guangxi province.

Across the road from the station exit a mob of taxis waited. Lined up with their drivers standing beside them, they looked like the start of the Monte Carlo Rally. The eager drivers waved and shouted enticements to the stream of prospective customers who surged through the gate. I was drawn to a couple of laughing young girls. They loaded me aboard with much merriment and didn't even try to cheat me.

The long-distance bus station was the usual mammoth affair with smelly trough toilets. My ticket to Yanshu cost two dollars sixty for the six hour journey and I only had half an hour to wait for the bus. I was sorely in need of a wash, but I thought, too bad, another six hours on a bus and I'll be worse.

In the station yard I saw one of the sleeper buses I had heard about. Two tiers of vinyl-covered benches interspersed with back rests were bolted into them. You could recline, but not lie flat. I was dubious about this mode of travel – the buses looked very top heavy and I'd heard that they had an alarming number of accidents. But I still had the urge to try this novel means of transport.

An announcement was made. The waiting horde surged to a locked gate where a guard stood behind a mesh screen and repelled all contenders except those who had the right bit of paper. She unlocked the gate and allowed the privileged few to pass through. I showed her my paper and made an attempt at the gate, but was repulsed back to my seat. The waiting crowd watched enthralled as this happened three more times (no wonder the Chinese think we are stupid) before I was finally admitted to the inner sanctum, the yard where the buses stood awaiting, and probably dreading, the onslaught of the passengers.

The bus, a large local job, did not move off until it had been packed sardine-full. As soon as we cleared the town the driver put his foot flat to the boards and the bus rocketed along, rattling over the rough dirt highway. My seat had been worn through to the metal and the edge became uncomfortable after a while. I couldn't open the window in front of me because it had a broken catch. It was not the worst bus I have been on, but I don't think Greyhound have much to worry about.

The other passengers were predominantly male. I had noticed that this was the norm in China, particularly in the younger age group. I supposed it was evidence of the one-child family program and the preference for boys. As usual the passengers smoked heavily and spat out of the windows or worse, inside the bus. My luggage was thrown up front near the driver where it was convenient for everyone to drop ash over it and put their feet on it. It survived the trip but came out absolutely filthy.

After Liuzhou there were towns and flat fields until we came to hills that were terraced and had cultivated plots in the valleys between them. Farmers wearing big saucer-shaped coolie hats dug potatoes, ploughed with buffalo or harvested grain. Here the hay stooks were shaped like little men wearing peaked hats. They marched across the fields looking like Cousin Id. Then mountains rose before us. Like nothing I had seen before, they were skinny and pointy, heavily wooded and dotted with patches of limestone. And what was this? The sun! I hadn't seen the sun for at least two weeks.

The sunshine made the bus pleasantly warm and the ride improved when we reached the mountains, as they slowed the driver considerably. It didn't stop his action on the horn though, a super-loud number that he blared every two seconds. But it did drown the voice of the woman behind me and gave a brief respite from her irritating discourse. She had started shouting to her neighbour, a complete stranger, the moment she got on the bus and she never let up for three-and-a-half hours, hardly drawing breath until she got off. Perhaps they didn't let her talk at home.

The scenery became wild and beautiful as we started climbing into the mountains. Eucalyptus trees with long white trunks rose sixty feet before their branches forked out; they looked as though they belonged in the Australian bush. We crossed several rivers and countless streams and stopped now and then to shovel more people into the bus even though there were no seats for them.

Three hours into our journey we pulled into a small bus station. The loo was another public exhibition job, although it did have small half doors that could be pulled across to cover the business end of you while leaving your head and shoulders on view. But by now I had become so blasé about displaying my charms to all and sundry I didn't see the doors until I was leaving. I didn't even look for a door. So much for my maidenly modesty.

I do not know the final destination of the bus I was on, but that is where I would have gone had I not recognised a sign in a town we were passing through. It was for a café called Minnie Mao's, which I had read was in Yanshu. How could I forget that? I showed my ticket to the driver and I think he said that, yes, this was Yanshu.

On terra firma once more, I was immediately accosted by a young woman who showed me a piece of cardboard with room prices crudely drawn on it. I showed interest and was promptly kidnapped. Shouting, 'Yes Yes!' the young woman, her accomplice and several assorted attendant females dragged me by the hand through the bus station, across the road and a hundred yards up the street to dump me in the Youth Hostel. This wasn't what I wanted. But it was now late afternoon and I had been travelling since four o'clock the previous morning.

Although I no longer cared where I stayed, I certainly arrived there in style. My entourage of six females herded me, giggling and chattering loudly (them not me), through the hostel's pavement café to make a grand entrance in reception. This seemed to greatly amuse a few westerners who sat outside. I felt a complete fool, but that was nothing new for me in China. The ladies deposited me with a gentleman who spoke excellent English and who graciously conducted me upstairs to inspect a room. It cost ten dollars and was the best bargain I had found so far. Clean and with no rodents in sight, the hostel seemed lovely after the last high-priced, rat-infested dump I had stayed in. By this time I was feeling extraordinarily jaded and all I wanted was to sit somewhere stationary and work on my fluid intake. I went down to the sidewalk café where twenty-six ounces of local, perfectly acceptable beer, cost me fifty cents.

The hostel was hippie heaven; great value rooms and lots of good, extremely cheap food and beer. You could even get your washing done for a few cents a piece. The laundry did not run to modern appliances – the washing machine took the form of a small Chinese woman – but it was so good to wear clothes that had been dried in the sunshine again.

Yanshu was a tourist village. In the time it took to imbibe my beer two charming ladies came to sit with me and try to induce me to take a tour with them. After the traumas of the rest of China, it was incredibly pleasing to find friendly people who spoke English, tried to help you, seemed to want you to be there and did not rip you off.

Although Yanshu is situated among rivers and mountains in the countryside, a dirty grey haze of pollution hung between the nearby mountain peaks and sat low on the village. But it was nowhere near as bad as that of the cities and the temperature was just right. The rainy season had just finished and the cold would come next.

In the morning I had an interesting 'American breakfast' outside on the pavement. It was alleged to consist of 'ham, sausages, eggs fired'. I got two very runny duck eggs that had been barely 'fired' and were sliding around a huge plate that had been decorated with a few microscopic bits of tinned, processed ham and a couple of slices of those awful red sausages, also 'fired'. Rock-hard toast kept this lot company. There was as much butter as you wanted (which was indeed a change, everywhere else it had been rationed like gold) and the coffee was good and strong, but I still decided that from then on it would be Chinese breakfast for me.

Then, as this was Sunday, I declared it to be a day of rest and did nothing except clean myself and my belongings. But there was no rest for my ears. A hideous noise assaulted me. Alternating Oriental music and political harangue blared from a loudspeaker on one side of the next building and across the road the drivers and touts at the bus station yahooed as they competed for custom.

In the evening I went for a walk. Yanshu was small enough to ramble all around and today was market day. From a large, under-cover market-place near the main street, stalls overflowed and spread out in lines that wound through the surrounding alleys and lanes. Most stalls sold clothing, fabrics and food. The lanes were lined with weathered grey or brown stone and mud-brick houses, many of them extremely old and tiny. Most of the houses were built around courtyards paved with ancient stones that had been polished smooth by hundreds of years of feet, or of earth packed to such a hard surface that it resembled terrazzo.

The traffic on the streets of Yanshu was sparse and mostly bike, motor-bike or converted tractor. Several forms of transport were available for those not inclined to walk. The most common was a push-bike affair with a contraption like a miniature covered wagon on the back. Or there was motor-bike transport on which you either rode pillion, or sat in a two seater side-car topped by a canvas awning. Many of the pedi-cab and motor-bike transport riders were young slim females; I had not seen this elsewhere in China. The alternative to all the above was to hire a bike and pedal yourself around.

The work-horses in the transport field were the modified tractors. They had a board at the front for the driver to sit on, another for his feet, and either half a van or a utility tray stuck on the back. A cross between the vehicles of Fred Flintstone and the Beverly Hill Billies, with a bit of lawn mower thrown in for good measure, they made more noise than the lot combined.

In the main street I was thrilled to discover an optician and a film processor (although the latter's produce proved dismal). A tourist inspired hair-dressing shop offered 'Head and Face washing and Blow to Head!' I hadn't had my face washed in years and didn't think I'd enjoy it any more now than I ever had. And as for the 'Blow to Head', they could forget that. What an offer. They wanted to scrub my face and then give me a clip over the ear to send me on my way. No thanks.

There was a music shop that would obligingly copy cassette tapes for you. Here there were no worries about copyright like there are in Hong Kong, where I got the fish eye and a disapproving glare when I asked for this service. There were also several dressmakers and, as my favourite pair of pants were about to give up the ghost I arranged for one establishment to make a copy of them. Other attractions of the street were old men with air guns who let you shoot half-blown-up balloons off a wall and itinerant sugar-cane sellers who would hack off the amount of cane you wanted on the spot. A pet monkey on a chain played in an open shop-front and animals, including owls, were for sale as food in the market. Knitters abounded. Using wooden or bamboo needles, they clacked away everywhere. I gave in and joined them, buying some wool and a set of needles made of bamboo. I may be a mechanical illiterate, but I am a champion knitter – and I have silver cups and show ribbons to prove it.

I noticed that the people of this district had darker skin and smiled more often than those of the north. And some of the old people were the smallest folk I had ever seen apart from pygmy Papua New Guinea Highlanders. Many were only the size of a ten-year-old. A few old people looked very poor and occasionally I saw an old soul in a patched pyjama suit wandering the streets. But I only saw one beggar; a leg-less young man who inched his way up the road on his hands and his stumps, pushing a money tin before him.

The main street also had many cafés, all of them with outdoor tables and seats to take advantage of the lovely weather. The prices at the cafés were all the same, very cheap. Whenever I sat down at a table someone would join me. At one café, the owner and the cook came to have a bowl of noodles with me and eventually they convinced me that I should go to visit a friend who was said to have some antiques. The café owner and I hopped into the side-car of a motor-cycle taxi and sped off down to the riverside wharf. But here I was disappointed to find only a row of stalls that sold mostly tourist rubbish, reproductions and fake antiques. No real antiques are for sale to the uninitiated in China. It is illegal to sell anything older than 150 years and that does not get you out of the Ching dynasty. The sellers wanted a fortune for anything even remotely old.

The stalls had sprung up on the river bank because this was where boats from up-market Guilin, eighty kilometres away up the River Li, off-loaded the hordes of package tourists who had made the trip down river to view the famous local scenery. The tourists were then returned to Guilin in the comfort of air-conditioned buses. For this privilege they paid 500 yuan. We lesser mortals, who chose to stay in down-market Yanshu, did the same trip in the opposite direction. Except that we went both ways by boat and took much longer, we saw the same sights for forty yuan.

Through Khai, the hostel manager, I arranged to go on this river trip one morning. After the usual hour's wait, I was marched to the wharf by a guide/keeper and plonked into a narrow wooden boat with an outboard motor, a driver-cum-captain and six other travellers. Then we waited some more while extra trade was drummed up along the wharf. Finally, with a complement of eight passengers and the bikes of those who wanted to ride back from one of the villages tied on the rear of the boat, we chugged off up the river.

Our guide spoke no English, which was a real help, but she had the happiest face I had seen in China. We sat two across in the boat on wooden chairs that looked like kindergarten escapees – microscopic pygmy seats for two-year-olds that were somehow reasonably comfortable.

Despite the clouds of pollution that hung around, it was a superb morning. The river was wide and, except in places where there was an eddy, its clear green water flowed placidly. In many spots the river-bank was lined by huge, but delicate, feathery bamboos. Small fish were jumping and, looking down, I saw that the water was shallow enough to see the stones on the river bottom – and the odd plastic container or bag that reposed among them.

The river and its edges were astir with life and activity. People fished from boats or the bank using big nets or small hand-held scoops. Sampans and houseboats went about their business, but the most common water transport were simple raft boats that were made by tying six thick bamboo poles with turned-up ends together. Boatmen did not sit on these flimsy-looking craft, they stood up and poled along. Cormorants tethered on wooden perches in the shallows waited for their night's fishing. Cormorants cost 1000 yuan and are very valuable servants. They are taken fishing after dark each night, and perch on one end of a raft boat while a woven basket for the fish sits on the other. The cormorant catches large quantities of fish, but a ring on his neck stops him swallowing them. Poor bird.

Water buffalo were being brought to the water's edge for their morning baths. Later, in the warm afternoon, we saw them standing contentedly with just their heads and necks sticking out of the river. Now and then a baby buffalo, too small to stand in the water, lay draped across his mother's back. Great flocks of village ducks roamed free and returned home under their own steam at night.

My fellow passengers included an interesting English couple who were working in Hong Kong, and their two well-behaved children. The boat's engine made a hell of an uproar, so all conversation was shouted. Everyone commented on the Chinese habit of spitting. I said, 'The day I get the urge to spit, that's the day I go home.' But I felt it was coming. All the pollution gave you a funny nose and throat.

We travelled a distance and then came to the mountains that make the scenery of this area of south China famous. I was now in the world of classical Chinese landscape paintings. The strangely shaped limestone peaks did not rise gently, there were no foothills or slopes leading up to them. They leaped long and thin straight out of the flat earth and sat alone, pointing to the clear blue sky. The unique formation of these moody mountains goes back several hundreds of million years to when this area was under the sea and an upheaval raised its status to that of dry land. Later it was flooded, then lifted again in more cataclysmic events. The alternating sea water and air created karst limestone formations that, vulnerable to erosion, evolved into pinnacles and caverns. Local people call them fascinating names – 'elephant trunk' and 'moon hill'. Thanks to the mountains' caves, Guilin and the surrounding district became the headquarters of those Chinese who resisted the Japanese during the second world war.

Our boat plodded on. We seemed to be the only one going in this direction, but after three hours we began passing boats that came from the opposite direction of Guilin. The trip up-river against the flow was slower than coming downstream, which was why the jet setters stayed in Guilin and did the trip vice versa.

The tourist boats were floating palaces compared to ours. They were loaded with fat cats dripping cameras, some of whom began photographing us. I thought this was weird, but then some tourists feel obliged to photograph everything in sight, even other tourists. Perhaps we looked colourful to them. The fat cats had, however, been fed. The hostel cook had offered me a sandwich to take with me. It had cost twice the regular price because it contained cheese. Kraft Cheddar, in fact. I was shown the label and told proudly, 'From Australia'. The slices of cheese tasted quite elderly and had been shaved off with a razor and put between thick old bread with no butter. Thank heavens I had not allowed the cook to toast it, as he had been determined to do, or it would have been a piece of rock.

Another hour later we turned around to come back. This was our first mistake. Our driver saw a mate on the shore who offered him some grapefruit. He took the boat in close to the shore to collect them and on the way back out we ran aground on some rocks. When I saw our captain start to take off his shoes I thought he was abandoning ship. No going down bravely with the vessel for him! But then he made us also take off our shoes and jump into a couple of feet of water to help him push the boat off. At last we freed the boat, but then it wouldn't steer straight. The rudder was bent. Back into the water we went again to push the boat to the shore. The captain got out the repair kit – consisting of one large hammer – and started to bang hell out of the rudder, which was merely a flat piece of cast iron. Then once again the passengers pushed the boat off.

In the meantime I had been ashore to avail myself of a bush. The riverbank was covered with tonnes of round weathered stones, a truck-load of which I would love to have taken home to build a garden wall. Several small, naked village boys approached me tentatively and stood at varying distances depending on their timidity. They looked ready to bolt at a second's notice, except for one – he was not afraid to come up and inspect me closely. Eventually the rest crept nearer, utterly engrossed with me, but none could be induced to smile. They were too busy absorbing my peculiarities.

Near the villages on the riverbanks, gangs of up to ten naked boys played in the water. We did not see one girl. Either they were all at home with their mothers learning how to cook, or there weren't any – maybe they had been drowned at birth. This is said to be still a common practice. There could be a problem in a few years time. Who would all these little boys marry?

Some of the small boys played chicken with the boats. This was very dangerous, as now and then they got caught between ours and a bigger boat going the other way. At one stage the captain indicated that the passengers who were sitting outside on the deck should throw their bags under cover. He knew what was coming. A pack of the little villains splashed waves of water at us. We all got wet, but the people out the front were soaked.

We approached Yanshu towards evening. Rows of sampans were moored on the banks near the village and on the deck of one I spied a man raising a hatchet to chop off his squawking dinner's head.

It was dusk when we alighted at the wharf. Strolling along winding lanes paved with rough cobblestones and lined with small shops, we made our way back to the hostel. By this time I was ravenous. I was thinking that I felt famished enough to eat a horse when I suddenly remembered, Oh

Lord! this was the night I had ordered a snake. Crikey, I muttered, not a horse, but I am going to have to eat a snake. Just as well I was hungry.

I had told a couple of people about this culinary adventure and when I came down to the street café an audience had gathered. They said that they had eaten early as they did not want to watch the horrible spectacle of me devouring a reptile while they had dinner. The cook asked me if I was ready for my snake and it was duly sent for. I imagined it would arrive already cooked and on a plate, but the snake was pedalled up to the curb, alive and kicking, in a flour bag in the front basket of an old lady's bike. The snake lady wore the old-fashioned, black, wide-legged trousers and side-buttoned jacket that old ladies still affected and her grey hair was neatly pinned in a bun. She felt around the outside of the flour bag for the business end of the snake, pinned it down, then put her other hand in the bag and, swapping hands, pulled the snake out and put in down on the ground in front of me.

My snake was about five feet long and it wriggled like mad, objecting strongly to this treatment. If it had known it was for dinner, it would have objected all the more. Grandma adroitly picked it up again by its head and offered it to me to play with. Not today thanks. Mother always told me not to play with my food and for once I was listening to her. The snake lady then produced a large pair of big handled scissors, took the snake to the gutter and – to the applause of the crowd of locals who had gathered – slowly cut off its head.

She bled the snake into the gutter, stripped out its entrails and skinned it. Then, holding it firmly – for the snake was still writhing and moving as strongly as it had done when alive – she put this twisting pinkish-grey, bare-fleshed thing under my nose and asked me how I wanted it cooked. Averting my eyes and keeping a firm grip on my stomach,

I mumbled that steamed would be fine, with lots of garlic.

Half an hour later my snake dinner appeared. The entire reptile, cleavered into two inch long bits, bones and all, lay on my plate. It was possibly only the thought of eating snake that was off-putting – the taste wasn't that bad. It was like chewy fish-cum-chicken. The only bad thing about the meal was trying to navigate safely around the splintered vertebra and rib bones. I had fortified myself for this test of my gastronomical courage with a large bottle of beer and I managed to eat the whole snake. I know the lot was on my plate because I found the little tail bit that didn't have any bones.

My meal caused much merriment among the friendly hostel staff and the resident westerners. I offered my delighted audience a taste, but I had no takers. Afterwards I wondered why I had done it. I had seen it on the menu and thought, why not. I had always found it intriguing that people of some cultures ate snakes and I wanted to see what it was like. I had not, however, much wanted to try a live one.

Eating snake is a virility trip to some Asians. (No, that was not why I wanted to try it.) Anything that is in any way shaped like a phallus is believed to give great potency. But it is usually only eaten by men. Goodness knows what the locals thought of my doing so. Maybe I gained a lot of face, or more likely they thought I was a most undesirable type of macho female. However, Khai told me I would be very strong tomorrow.

The hostel had good vibes. My large room had walls so roughly plastered that they appeared to have been done by a blind man in the dark, but it was comfortable. And there was not one single rat in the bed with me at night. What more could a girl ask? There was even hot water. I had my own personal little water heating system, the mysteries of which Khai explained to me. They were quite something.

First you turned on a gas cylinder that sat in one corner of the bathroom. The gas connected to a small instant hot water heater that you turned on next. Then, by pulling a lever and banging up and down on a wrench that was attached to a pipe that emerged through a hole in the wall, you hoped to produce hot water. There were no taps. A tin basin was strategically placed underneath the shower to catch the drips. Why just this one drip was considered worthy of such attention was a puzzle. Everything else simply leaked onto the floor regardless.

The narrow attached bathroom was institution-sized. You entered it by climbing up two steps from the bedroom and immediately encountered a half wall that had been placed there for an obscure reason. At one end of the room was a hand-basin that looked as though it had been installed with a shovel and a loo that coursed water all the time, but still managed to flush. A length of fencing wire attached to screws that had been banged into each end wall dangled the length of the room to serve as a towel rail. A long narrow window ran along the outside wall. It contained one pane of glass, then had a four-inch gap followed by another piece of glass. Obviously there had not been enough glass to fit the lot.

Opposite the hostel was a park in which a ludicrously tall thin mountain, on whose top a tiny pagoda perched, zoomed straight up out of nowhere. My room was almost on a level with this pagoda and my bathroom window, innocent of curtains, looked straight at it. I swore that if it housed a monk he would be able to see right in. Maybe the hotel staff sent him a flash when a female was in residence.

Despite the bathing refinements provided, I still had cold showers two mornings running. The first morning I soaped my hair and stepped under the shower before I discovered that the gas bottle was empty. The second morning I found I could not regulate the heat of the water. Finally I got the hang of it, but it was a bit of a worry. When in use the system would give a little pop every now and then. That was the warning that the water was about to run cold for ten seconds. I learned to hop aside on this omen and wait for the water to warm up again.

A constant hideous noise emitted from the bathroom. It originated in the exhaust fan that Khai had told me I should leave on at all times. When he had been instructing me in the intricacies of the hot water service, I had asked, 'Isn't this dangerous. What if the gas bottle leaks?' He blithely replied, 'No problem. This is why you have this.' And he pulled a cord that set the exhaust fan off in an awful row. 'And you leave this go all the time in case the gas leaks – so, no problem, no problem.'

The first time I used the hand-basin I felt water splash on my feet and looked down to see that instead of the plumbing pipe trailing off into the great unknown as was usual, it ended a foot from the floor. Water fell from it, then flowed along the sloping incline of the tiles to the end of the room, where it disappeared down a convenient hole in the floor. Very cute, I thought, but where does it go from there – to the bathroom on the floor below?

I had a large, comfortable bed, a couple of small cupboards and another piece of wire looped across the room to constitute a wardrobe. There were even bed lights, pulled on by tiny chains. An endless supply of hot water for tea, coffee or noodles was readily available. You took your thermos downstairs and swapped it for one of those that were lined up waiting outside the kitchen door.

My room was on the top (or second) floor. On one side my neighbours were three friendly blond Danish boys and on the other, two very tall Swedish fellows. The door of my room opened onto a long narrow verandah, equipped with cane chairs at the back of the hostel. Here I could sit and contemplate a skinny mountain that rose to a great height directly in front of the verandah, or watch local life below in the courtyard between the hostel and two apartment blocks in which Chinese families lived. These buildings were the usual flat-roofed rectangular boxes but they were cheered up by rows of window planters in which bright red geraniums flowered. The buildings' roofs had no rails or edges and sometimes I saw the occupants walking around on them which made me, with my fear of heights, feel quite ill.

I put my undies, face washer and then my feet on the balcony rail; the weak sun was delightfully warm on my bare skin. Under my feet a small boy babbled, children played and grandpa minded the baby while mother worked. Grandma collected citrus peel from the streets and gutters and spread it out on the ground to dry. This was a local cottage industry. I learned that the peel was sold to manufacturers of Chinese medicine.

Every Saturday night at dusk the air in the street outside the hostel was blasted asunder by a great salvo of firecrackers. I was glad to hear that this was to clear the bad spirits away for the weekend. It was a good idea. But I noticed that it was done conspicuously near the hostel. It was probably thought that the profusion of big noses in there encouraged bad spirits.

6 Cops and Robbers

One afternoon a few days later found me lying on my bed
with my leg up on a pillow resting my throbbing wounds and
recovering from what had been a difficult morning. Apart
from minor irritations, I had been robbed, fallen off a bicycle
and had several brushes with death.

That morning I had been indulging in a leisurely outdoor
breakfast at the hostel's café when I decided to hire a
bicycle. I hadn't ridden a bike for years and I was never
any good at it, so I am not sure what madness came over me.
I will leap confidently onto any four-legged animal, but
bicycles and I just don't get along. I have scars on my knees
to prove it. And now I had acquired a couple more to add to
my collection. (Although the bigger of the new ones actually overlapped the scar I got two years ago when I fell off
the table on which I was dancing at the sailing club after the
Darwin Cup – but that is another story.)

Looking over the line of bicycles at the kerb-side, I chose
a machine whose pretty colour matched the purple trim on
my hat. The hirer assured me that this was a good bicycle as
I paid the eighty cents fee. I told him that I did not know
how to ride a bike with gears and he said that it did not
matter because the gears were broken anyway. I tied on my
hat, had the cracked and broken seat adjusted to my height,
shoved my bag in the front basket and wobbled shakily
away from the kerb. A woman tout rode close on my rear
wheel and tried to induce me to take a boat trip. Shouting

desperately, 'Get out of my way!' I teetered around the island in the middle of the road. Then I discovered that I did not know which side of the road to take. I chose the wrong one and after reeling up the street against the oncoming traffic, I made a very dangerous turn. Motor-bikes sheared off in all directions, narrowly missing me. Wobbling along in the gutter I decided that my bike was unstable. It wasn't just a case of a poor workman blaming his tools, as my dad would have said, the machine was terribly shaky and the handle bars seemed to be loose. I weaved up to the shop I wanted to visit and put the brakes on sharply. The front wheel hit the curb with a bang and the bloody bike threw me! Just like a horse, it chucked me up into the air and I came down in a four point landing on the concrete footpath. I got up, dusted myself off and swore furiously at the bike. I had a bleeding knee, my jeans were in tatters and so was my dignity.

My business with the shop completed, I set off again. The touting woman still pursued me. Now she wanted me to ride out into the country with her. I told her to go away. I was having quite enough trouble with the main street without contemplating the rugged countryside outside Yanshu with its rough dirt tracks and steep hills. Weaving into the tangle of bikes and motor bikes that made up the main stream of traffic, I somehow made it to the other end of the town.

Arriving at my destination, I fell off. It seemed to be the only way I could get off this rotten invention. At least this time I landed on soft ground, but I went down sideways with the bike on top of me and got very dirty. After an hour of this I came home a grisly sight. Mulga Bill's bike had nothing on this renegade crate. I had hit a motorbike, a pedi-cab, two pedestrians and another pushbike and only escaped the jaws of death under the wheels of every vehicle I had come near by a hair's breadth. I was a nervous wreck by the time I finally gave up, dismounted, and walked the rest of the way back to the hostel.

'You can have this bloody bike back,' I told the bike's custodian. Laughing uproariously, he handed me my eighty cents. The hostel staff all thought it was a great joke, but I refused to unfluff my feathers and went off in a huff.

I finished what I had to do on foot, soothing and fortifying myself with a couple of feeds along the way. It was hard not to eat continuously in Yanshu, as everywhere you went there were side-walk cafés offering enticing dainties. Mickey Mao and Minnie Mao ran rival cafés, but both served Big Mao Burgers, whatever they were. I had a Chinese version of a pizza at Minnies. It tasted good but had the consistency of crockery. I was unable to get my knife into it, so I smashed it up and ate it with my fingers.

At the end of the village the road passes between two peaky mountains that seem to be closely guarding it. Then it crosses over a bridge and goes out to the surrounding villages. Along the edges of the road a street market was in progress. I walked down the long line of sellers who had vegetables, fruit and clothing set out on the ground. One man had three hessian bags containing various grades of tobacco. He did not look like a grower and he certainly wasn't a rep from Rothmans. I think his tobacco came from butts recycled out of the gutter. On several occasions I had seen a tiny, humped-backed old lady in a big coolie hat and black pyjamas picking up cigarette ends from the gutters with a pair of wooden tongs and dropping them into a wicker basket. Another vendor was sound asleep alongside his bundles of freshly picked herbs, another offered to cure you with the potions he would prescribe on the spot, and an old man told fortunes with his red-figured horoscope chart.

Investigating behind the main road I discovered minute lanes that led into the original part of the village. Here ancient houses huddled together in clusters and open drains seemed to be the only means of sanitation. I wandered back along the road and turned into a side street that looked like a short cut to the wharf. I had not gone far when I was jostled from behind and felt someone touch the large shopping bag that was slung over my shoulder. A young man sped past me. He had a grey jacket draped over his head, as men sometimes did here to keep the sun off the back of their necks. But in this case it looked suspicious, and I thought I saw him whisk something up under the coat as he went off at a terrific lick. I stopped immediately and looked in my bag. My purse was gone. And so was he, long gone. So it was no use screaming or shouting. I was not unduly upset about my loss – it had only been sixty dollars and my bus ticket to Guangzhou – but I was most annoyed with myself for being so stupid. Even though my purse had been in the bottom of the bag and not on the top, I shouldn't have carried it in an open receptacle. The thief must have seen me put it there when I had paid for my lunch and he had probably been stalking me ever since. Because there were few people about, I had dropped my guard. At the neighbouring village of Fuli's market, which attracts huge crowds and is a notorious haunt of pickpockets and thieves, I would have clutched my money closely to me or had it stuffed under my clothes.

I crept home to my room defeated by this day. There wasn't much else I could do. I had no money, a sore leg and I was thoroughly cheesed off. On the way back to the hostel I asked the owner of the café the location of the police station. He told me it did not open until three o'clock. Too bad if murder, pillage and rapine were going on down in the town during siesta time.

Khai was very upset when I told him about the theft and gave me a long lecture about keeping my money around my neck. My American cash dollars and travellers cheques were safely hidden in my room however, so I was able to change some money with him.

But wait! There's more! The day was not over yet. After a morning of bike accidents and purse pinching I had the ordeal of the police. I took a motorbike taxi to the police station where I found an office occupied by a nice young man who, with his limited English and a phrase-book, did his best to help me. We got through the preliminaries and past the obstacle of his thinking that I was left destitute after my loss and had no other money. 'Do you have friends who can help you?' Finally convincing him that the sixty dollars I had lost was not my life savings and only means of support, we went on to fill out many forms. Then I had to write a report and copy it by hand three times. There was no carbon paper.

Now the real problem surfaced. It seemed that the stamp and the certificates to prove that I had made the report I needed for an insurance claim were in the cupboard and like everything else in China the cupboard was securely pad-locked. And the key to the cupboard was missing. 'Have you notified the police?' I quipped. 'Ho ho. You should fill out a report.' The policeman laughed, genuinely amused.

It turned out that the key was with the boss who might or might not return that day. My friend tried to phone this man and then we waited. I knitted and helped the policeman polish his English. Time passed. There were more phone calls. I was asked to come back in a couple of days when the investigations would be over. 'What investigations?' I asked. 'I just want a claim form for the insurance and I am leaving for Guangzhou soon.'

Another western traveller drifted in. He was also asked to wait. He had been told to return on this day for his visa extension. A skinny Frenchman who was pedalling a bike around the world, he informed me that he had been eight months getting this far across China. I said, 'How do you manage when you get to whacking big mountains like the ones around the Great Wall?' He replied, 'Eet eez just ze same as you 'ave ze car. You just change ze gears and up ze mountain you go.' I did not let on that I could not change ze gears. I could not even get around ze first corner without coming ze cropper. He eventually left saying he would get his extension in the next town.

Then, in a storm of discord, the Holder of the Key arrived. He roared around the room wafting an overpowering trail of booze behind him. His face was very red as he shouted, boy how he shouted, and yelled. He staggered to the table and read, or pretended to read, my report. Then he slurred questions at me, 'When did you come here? How long have you been here? Where are you going?' I was getting the third degree and I was the victim! Then things got nasty. I was not registered as an alien in town. He shoved a form that listed the names of the law-abiding foreigners who had done so under my nose and demanded to know why I had failed to let the police know that I was staying at the youth hostel. Unfortunately Khai, the hostel manager, had omitted to pass on this information.

Eyeing me all the time with deep suspicion, he continued to ask me irrelevant questions. Then came the final crunch that convinced him I was indeed a dangerous type and up to no good in China. 'Where is your customs form?' I didn't have one. As I had arrived in China by ship, it had somehow been overlooked. He said, 'If you had one you could prove you had this money you *say* you lost. How do we know you had it at all.' His puffy face, already suffused with grog and rage, got even redder. His eyes narrowed to slits as he pushed his face close to mine. It was not a pretty sight. As he tried to speak he slavered, slurring so badly that he was actually chewing his words and spitting them out complete with flecks of saliva, some of which fell on my face.

I tried to explain the illogic of his question; that the money I lost would not have been the same money that I brought into the country and therefore would not have been identifiable, as I had been exchanging traveller's cheques all along the way. He seized the phone, dialled the hostel and screamed at Khai, who, thank heavens, must have vouched for me and done his best to convince this drunk tyrant that I was not evil.

After much more bluster from Nasty Pants, the young man unlocked the cupboard and laboriously filled out the loss form, stamped it with an impressive red seal, made millions of copies by hand and attempted to give one to me. But Nasty Bugger stopped him, demanding ten yuan. I said, 'I have no money. I just had it all stolen!' Adding under my breath, 'By another thief.' I did actually have money. I just wasn't going to give it to this creep. He refused to let me have the form without paying. I got stubborn and said, 'I'll come back tomorrow.' Meanwhile, while Nasty was busy ranting, the nice policeman caught my eye and slowly and unobtrusively slid the form across the desk in my direction. I inched it off the desk behind Nasty's back and slipped it into my bag. The Nice Person nodded to me to take off. I sidled out and bolted down the road, half expecting to be pursued, apprehended and locked up at any minute. Halfway along the road the Nice Person – I'd heard about the good cop and the bad cop routine, but this was ridiculous – pedalled up on his bike. He dismounted and walking beside me escorted me to the main street, charmingly making tentative apologies for his odious mate.

At the corner he left me and I walked on alone. Beneath my calm 'face' I was in a state of shock. I went to report a crime and I got investigated and interrogated! A display of local gut-rot booze on the street caught my attention. Just what I needed to sedate my nerves. For one dollar thirty cents I bought a litre of something that turned out to be remarkably like dry cleaning fluid, which I mixed with some of the delicious, fresh squeezed mandarin orange juice that the café provided. It was a sin to pollute such beautiful stuff with this poison and it tasted frightful. Now that *was* a crime I should have been arrested for. A glass of this concoction imbibed before and after my dinner was all I could manage. I still had nine hundred millilitres left to dispose of, but I could not face another of shot of petrol!

I reflected that I was in loss mode. Today I had also lost my sun glasses. I put them down on the counter of a shop and they disappeared, poof, like magic. Yesterday I had left my camera case on the top of a mountain and I certainly wasn't climbing back up to retrieve it. My faith in the inherent goodness of man had taken a severe battering since I had come to China. It was in intensive care at the moment, still alive, but only just.

That night in bed when I closed my eyes I could still see the face of Nasty Pants. And in my sleep the revelation came to me that China was a place not to be enjoyed but endured.

Talking to other travellers, I had found that many did not think that China was a country they would want to visit again. The hostility, prejudice, discrimination and rip-off foreigner prices thoroughly bugged them. One German couple said that they had come for six months, but were leaving after six weeks. An American man had come for three months and left after ten days. And there were many other similar stories.

One night at a café I met the first Australian I had seen in a long time. He was the only person who said that he would like to return to China, but then he had only been in the south and to Dali, which is another hippie heaven. I would have liked to know what he thought after he had travelled in the north.

I agreed with the general opinion that Yanshu was Okay. Yanshu was a back-packer's haunt and the local people had got used to weird western ways. The drawback to Yanshu, which was full of travellers, was the mob of touts who continually hassled you. The staff of the youth hostel were extremely cordial and helpful and actually knew something about the rest of their country. So did the small local office of CITS. I couldn't believe my ears when I was told this. But Murphy's law saw to it that this was the one place I did not need advice. I had arranged a berth on a sleeper bus to Guangzhou absolutely painlessly through Khai at the hostel.

I spent a morning in the park opposite the hostel. At the ornate gate, I was asked to pay one hundred and twenty times the price the locals paid. For this extortion I received a pretty postcard ticket. The park was one of the few peaceful places I found in China. Leafy trees shaded concrete paths flanked by stone-edged garden beds, while on the grass, small stone stools surrounded stone tables like a fairy ring of mushrooms. Some senior citizens played crochet; others minded tiny tots. That seemed to be a very good system – put the very old and the very young together to take care of each other. It beats child care centres. Under spreading trees, hopeful fishermen dangled their lines from the walled edges of a big, clear pond that was fed by the river. A group of old men sat in an open-sided pagoda soaking up the sun and playing cards. An old lady invited me to join her in some tai chi. Thank goodness tai chi is universal. I have had ten lessons in sum total, but I did my best to keep up with her. She was a champ.

I climbed three hundred or so steps to the top of the park's skinny hill and reached the pagoda that was at eye level with my bathroom. The steps, which were overshadowed by trees and foliage, had been cut into the rock and, with their worn and crumbling edges, felt unsafe in places. The tiny pagoda had stone seats around its open walls for visitors to rest on and look out over the countryside. I flopped down to lower my pulse rate. Surveying the condoms and cigarette packets under my feet, I was surprised that anyone had had the energy to indulge in either of these pursuits after those coronary inducing stairs.

One day I came across the local dentist at work and I was

grateful then that at least in Chungking I'd had an inside job. In Yanshu the dentist had a tiny office where the torture chair was strategically placed in the middle of a large window that fronted the main street. The victim had to face crowds of fascinated onlookers, who lined up outside, only millimetres away, to watch the fun. It was better entertainment than the pictures and much cheaper. What an audience I'd have drawn.

I visited another clinic to enquire about some anti-malarial tablets. In a grotty hole, an unqualified practitioner offered massage and other cures for ten yuan and prescribed and dispensed pills without a licence. He also did some dentistry and calmly interrupted our discourse to pull a tooth. No anaesthetic was given and no attempt was made to save the tooth of the young woman. She was a stoic; she did not even flinch. The 'dentist' used unsterile pliers for the operation, thus giving the patient a good chance of acquiring septicaemia. She spat out a stream of blood onto the floor. I left.

At the hostel I'd had a change of neighbours and, now, when I relaxed on my balcony in the evening, a pair of Chinese tourists from Hong Kong sat close by. He was a round chain-smoking butterball and his girlfriend must have been hilarious. He shrieked in a high-pitched giggle at every word she uttered. She, however, had nothing to smile about. Although she was dainty and smartly dressed, he was unattractive to an extreme degree. His teeth were like crooked washboards you could have driven a truck between and he had tiny piggy eyes. Sick of his noise, I concluded waspishly that he must have had some well hidden attribute like a large wallet.

Some evenings rifle shots rang out from the side of the mountain that faced me on the balcony and I saw ant-sized figures moving on the path that wound around its densely wooded slope. Another endangered species for the pot.

The surrounding villages took turns to hold their markets

and on the morning that the village of Fuli had theirs I set off to visit it by small boat. Although Fuli was only five kilometres away by road, it took an hour to chug down the river lazily. It was a glorious morning and the other passengers, two German boys, sat in the soft sun on the deck of the prow and played Chinese chess with round checkers.

The river's still waters reflected the beauty of the mountains and buffalo stood ankle deep in the shallows. Maybe it was too cold for further insertion just yet. Men in small boats harvested water-weed for animal food and women squatted at the water's edge to beat their washing on flat rocks. Occasionally a water carrier came down to dip his two wooden buckets in the river and move off with them swinging on the yoke across his shoulders.

We landed on the riverbank opposite Fuli, and I stepped from stone to stone across the rocks that made a path through the shallows to the other side. Reaching the rough-hewn stone landing, I climbed a lofty flight of steps to the top of the bank where, shaded by colossal old trees, a pretty pagoda looked down on the river. From here a narrow cobbled lane, lined by tiny old wooden houses with tiled roofs, meandered round before it reached the centre of the village high on a hill. Most of the houses consisted of only one room with wooden shutters that opened onto the street across its front. Most shutters were open to the sun and I could see that the houses were frugally furnished with wooden stools and low tables. One house sported a big picture of Chairman Mao surrounded by other deities. Some dwellings were being used as warehouses, or for cottage industries. In one I saw a girl treadling an old-fashioned sewing machine and in another, wool was being spun. Women sat on stools in their doorways. Some knitted, one young mother fed a bald baby noodles with chopsticks. I noticed that all the people of this district wore conical straw hats and traditional clothes. Outside the barber shop a young man washed his hair in a red plastic bucket – that must have been the shampoo service. There was obviously no running water or electricity.

I reached the market; a long, narrow cement floor flanked by concrete pillars that held up a peaked roof under which were housed several avenues of stalls. Throngs of people slowly wended past the goods – clothing, shoes, wool, buttons, bows and gegaws – which were displayed on benches or on the ground. In the press of bodies, I moved as fast as I could through the meat section, another of those places it was best not to dawdle in. The poisons department, positioned conveniently next to the food, offered bottles and packets of lethal potions, as well as a tastefully arranged display of large dead rats as proof that they worked. There were also medicines that I concluded must be for your afflicted buffalo. A munificence of fruit and vegetables was exhibited, as well as sacks and baskets of every kind of grain and lentil imaginable. And a marathon array of an unbelievable variety of spices, condiments, herbs and Chinese medicines were lined up neatly in tiny hessian bags with their tops turned down. Next came all kinds of dried plants and animals and stacks of dried ducks, as flat as pancakes, which were the colour of dirty tan shoes and looked just as tasty.

The stalls overflowed the market place and ran along the lanes on either side of it. Bright cheery cheeps from day old chicks and ducklings that were only tiny balls of golden fluff led me to the live goods area, where big ducks quacked under wicker baskets. Someone squeezed past me holding a brace of squawking brown hens upside down by the feet – dinner on the hoof. A man pulled a small hand cart through the crowd, on which six large, pink and white pigs encased in woven bamboo cocoons were stacked in two layers. They were surprisingly quiet for pigs in this undignified position. If you have ever heard a pig venting his displeasure at being interfered with, you will know what I mean.

A watch mender sat on a stool in front of a microscopic stand that contained his accoutrements of trade and performed emergency surgery on a timepiece while its owner breathed down his neck. A boot mender also did on the spot re-furbishings. I bought a replacement for the purse I had lost and a comb from an old lady who squatted on the ground with a small rattan tray on her lap. Whenever possible, I bought from street vendors. I decided that they needed the money more than the government who owned all the big shops. Walking on, I left the market behind and followed the winding lane through the village until the houses thinned out and I came to a cross road. On the outskirts of the village, where vegetable gardens and patches of crop were being hand watered with buckets, a motorbike taxi waited.

I negotiated a return ride to Yanshu in this smart conveyance. It had bright red paint and a green frilled canvas canopy that covered both passenger and driver. I climbed in the side-car. The driver's girlfriend hopped on the pillion and we rode slowly along the tree-fringed road through countryside that was dotted with stooks of hay and planted with vegetables, bamboo and rice. The side-car had enough room for two small bottoms and halfway along the road we picked up two girls. One got in with me to practise her English; the other took the place of the driver's girlfriend on the pillion. The girlfriend then sat on the mudguard of the side-car and braced her feet on the step. The RTA would have had a fit, but it was very cosy and we all parted friends.

In Fuli I had seen a couple of families who appeared to have two children. Out here in the country it must be easier to get away with having more than the one child allowed – if you could escape the notice of the dreaded Baby Police. These uniformed characters, who rank on a level with the Gestapo in the popularity polls, prowl the villages in motorcycle side-cars, hunting out families who have more than their ration of children. The male partner found guilty of this heinous offence is immediately taken to the nearest hospital for a vasectomy, as well as being heavily fined and penalised. I was told the story of one man who was found to have produced three children. After being apprehended and put in the side-car for the hospital trip, he jumped from the vehicle and, hitting his head on the concrete gutter, was left there unconscious on the side of the road. He died. Some birth control!

After two weeks of rest and recuperation in Yanshu, it was time to move on to Guangzhou. By this time I had won a heart – Khai, the hostel manager, who told me I walked like a mannequin. Me! Whom my dad used to call Tanglefoot and say I'd trip over the pattern on the carpet. I couldn't wait to tell my relatives, who say I walk like a ruptured duck. This near-sighted gent asked if I had formerly been a model. A model of what? And formerly? In a former life? Love is surely blind! Khai was unusual for a Chinese. He was a chubby, cuddly type with a round happy face, round glasses and receding hair that added to his cuddly look. He described himself as, 'the fat man with glasses, half bald'. He was a cheerful friendly man who, despite his westerni-sation, still had a spit now and then. At least he walked over to the gutter to do it.

The sleeper bus was a great disappointment. I had seen them standing empty in the bus station where they looked quite civilised, but that was before the Chinese got stuck into them. I had been warned. At the hostel I met three Englishmen who had just arrived from Guangzhou on a sleeper bus. They said the trip had been a nightmare. The stereo blasted full bore in their ears the entire journey, the driver had blown the horn every three seconds and almost all of the road was under construction.

At three in the afternoon Khai carried my bags to the bus station. There it stood, the oldest sleeper bus on the market.

Tatty and careworn, it looked like a zoo cage from the outside. Through its tinted windows all you could see were bars – the supports for the upper berths and the rungs for climbing up to them. Double decker sleepers were fixed along each side of the bus as well as down the middle where they were flanked by two very narrow aisles. Across the back were crammed two layers of five berths in which the customers lay like rows of sardines.

We started off with the bus only half full of passengers, six of whom were foreigners. As we drove through the pretty country outside Yanshu the conductor issued us with a doona each. I rolled mine into a bolster to prop myself up and knitted. You couldn't sit, so I travelled sprawled back like the Queen of Sheba rolling through her domain.

We passed more of the mountains peculiar to this locality that stuck up like fingers growing straight out of the ground. Everywhere I looked I saw people in the fields bringing in the harvest, while children played under the watchful eyes of their grandparents. In the villages fruit was laid out on racks and tables to dry, and rice was spread on the ground or being winnowed. Now and then we passed a large pig going home on a bicycle – not riding it, but hanging over both sides in an open-weave, wicker basket. And most definitely alive, as evidenced by the stream of fluid that emitted outwards from the business end of one to hit the side of our bus. One bicycle even had two pigs on it. Another bore an army of chooks in two tiers of wire cages. A regular bus passed us with a ludicrous looking load tied on its roof; a three-seater sofa atop an awkward and unstable pile of motley baggage. I reflected that this was the ultimate way to travel; taking your own seat with you. In one village the bus swerved to miss a puppy, not a pet, but someone's dinner. It was the only dog I had seen alive in China so far.

We had only driven a short distance from the bus station when we were hailed by a group of people who were waiting by the side of the road, all packed and ready to travel. After they had spent fifteen minutes arguing and shouting with the driver and the conductor, I wondered testily why they couldn't have booked a ticket. The crew finally decided to take them on board. The main concern seemed to have been the establishment of the fare. From then on this performance was repeated every few kilometres until midnight when, after much squeezing, shouting and shoe-horning, we had been finally jam-packed to our maximum capacity. By then the aisles were a climb-over job and the front of the bus was stacked high with cargo. It took an incredible amount of fuss to get people allocated places. Wondering what they could possibly be going on about for so long and in such a convoluted manner, I decided that they all must be a bit thick.

One group's luggage included many large fodder bags tied at the neck, one of which was moving suspiciously. Some of this baggage went up on the roof, but most came inside the bus. The female of the group negotiated with the driver's mate and the conductor, who prodded all the bags to suss out their contents. But when the conductor turned away for a moment, two more huge bags were manoeuvred on to the bus from behind a wall. One of the men got in the bus and opened my window so that the woman could pass the stuff up to him. He then hauled these grotty old bags over me, my bedding, and my bags. Towards evening we passed another sleeper bus. It was lying on its side in the rice paddy.

Just on twilight we pulled into a wayside stop for dinner. It was a rough sort of shed that was open to the road at the front and contained low wooden tables and Lilliputian, kindy chairs. I ate chicken and green chilli peppers, hot and tasty, while watching a mauve, pink and purple sunset streak the sky. Then it was dark – and how! There had been a power failure. Candles were produced, but they were obviously cooking with coal as food still continued to be supplied. Tripping downstairs to the loo, I found a damp wet dungeon, and then it was back on the road.

The bus was now mostly full of Chinese men, all of whom chain-smoked, spat and blew their noses – I didn't want to know where – they had no hankies and they did not open a window. My berth was the last one in front of the double row of bunks across the rear where the occupants lay smoking and shouting to each other. I began to feel the effects of inhaling so much nicotine, but the fresh air fiends of day time buses, who put all the windows down and blew your head off, converted after dark to wimps who were convinced that the night air kills. The bus remained shut tight as a drum and the air inside became progressively foggier and foggier. Cigarette butts and ash were dropped inside the bus rather than out the window. When I opened my window, the man behind me pushed it shut. The man directly above me hung the hand that held his cigarette down level with my eye until I took his wrist and gently pushed it up. He took the hint, but still flicked ash down onto the people and the boxes and bags below. Finally his still lighted butt descended, he cared not where.

The road was as appalling as I had been warned. Detours continued for hundreds of miles and at one of them we were held up for over an hour. The road was not being repaired in small sections; the whole lot was being done at once. Then our bus suffered a breakdown and we sat on the side of the road for another hour.

In the front of the bus next to the driver was a flat bench on which the co-driver slept. Despite the bumpiness of the road and the hours of detours I also had some sleep, but it was full of vivid and strange dreams. At one stage I woke and, looking up blearily, I saw a man I thought was the driver outlined in front of me. Then to my absolute horror I saw him lie down flat. I was in shock before I realised that the driver was on the other side.

Four hours after dinner we had a comfort stop by the side of a dark piece of road and I had to perform what is normally a private affair among hundreds of men. By this time I didn't care. Even when I got caught with my pants down by a truck coming slowly up the hill with its lights on high beam I wasn't phased. China is a great leveller.

7 The Bike Police

Guangzhou straddles the Pearl River, the fifth longest river in China, which links the city to the South China Sea and is thronged with ferries, freighters, junks, sampans, small tankers and big gun boats. Foreigners have been coming to Guangzhou, as they called China's first major seaport, for a couple of thousand years. Established around 200 BC and the capital of the Guangdong Province for over a thousand years, it is one of China's largest cities. By the end of the Han Dynasty, in 200 AD, foreign trade linked the port with other areas of Asia, as well as India and the Roman Empire. By the ninth century a large colony of Arabs, Jews and Persians had settled here to trade in silk, tea and porcelain. In the sixteenth century, Europeans came to Guangzhou. First the Portuguese, then the Spanish, Dutch and English, who set up trading posts in the late eighteenth century. Now, although Guangzhou is primarily an industrial city, it is still involved in making money and hustling.

At six o'clock in the morning, our bus pulled into Guangzhou. It was still dark, and I had no idea where I was. Only the main bus station was marked on my map, and this was not it. A couple of English blokes, who had also been on the bus, and I lined up with a bunch of local workers in the station café for some breakfast noodles. Later I realised that the twelve yuan I had paid had been for all three of our breakfasts. The boys had paid as well. But a refund was out of the question. The cashier was programmed to take money, not give it back.

Mark, John and I decided to travel to the Guangzhou Youth Hostel together. Yanshu had been my first experience of hostels, and I had formed a good opinion of them. Three taxi drivers turned us down before we found one who could read the map we were using to indicate our destination. At the hostel, the boys paid to leave their luggage – they were going to Hong Kong that night by train – and I put my name on the waiting list for a room. I was told to come back at check out time. I went to a café across the road from where I could keep an eye on the hostel. When I saw the night receptionist leave, I returned to stake my claim with the day staff. You see how much I had learned! Then I moved to the hostel's café. Adjacent to the foyer, it was closer for a speedy ambush if I saw guests departing.

At ten o'clock I spied people leaving, so I presented myself at the reception desk. Here I discovered that the staff were not keeping rooms for those they had written on the waiting list. I caught them in the act of admitting several middle-aged Chinese who had just trickled in. And this was supposed to be a youth hostel.

Other travellers had told me that Guangzhou was a ghastly place, but I was favourably impressed with it. Later I wondered if I had enjoyed Guangzhou because it was not totally Chinese! The youth hostel is situated on Shamian Island, a small residential area that was formerly the colonial foreign enclave, and is linked to the city by two bridges. The island retains the peaceful ambience of the nineteenth century and staying here was what helped me to appreciate Guangzhou. The streets are lined with beautiful old buildings that have been carefully restored. Lovely big banyan trees hang over the cobbled footpaths that are bordered by gardens edged with low concrete walls topped by white iron fences. The hostel is housed in one of the fine old buildings and looks nothing like I imagined a youth hostel should.

It was no mean feat, but I did finally get a small room on the fourth floor of the hostel. The first thing I noticed in the room was a large document that was pasted in a prominent position on the wall. 'Youth Hostel Rules,' it read.

We hope that you will be comfuble and safe stay in Youth Hostel in this case we will proceate your co operation number one etc or you will get a fine.

If you loose your registration card you will had to pay two yuan compensation

Only water washing. (??)

Please swiss off lights and lock windows

Articles in room were for use only not for momento to be taken away

Please don't dismantle the electricle appliances and equipments otherwise compensation must be paid according to price

Were not allowed to bring in inflamable explosive poisons radio active materials livestock rancid materials

You should not cook food light a fire or explode fire crackers in room as well as smoke in bed a fine of 30 will be issued to voilaters

Visiting protitution drug taking and gambling in room strictly forbidden voilaters will be punished according to Chinese law

Keep your room tidy don't spit to the floor litter cigarette ash and end as well as rind and groceries pour tea into wrong place don't put tea bags into wash basin or below but dust bin don't pour water out from windows if having done so you will be punished according to the corcerning the regulations

Please pay attention to your appearance when leaving the room don't wrap yourself with sheet and quilt cover

Visitors were required to register at reception those who come for visit after eleven Pm are not welcomed

Please don't make confused noise or play card after ten Pm

A couple personns who are opposite sex grown ups who want to live in same room must had a legal marriage permit.

A list of fines payable as compensation for anything that went missing followed. And heaven forbid that anyone should be so depraved as to want to take away the hostel rules. That crime would cost you fifty cents.

The hostel had recently been re-vamped after a massive fire (firecrackers, smoking in bed, exploding radioactive devices, or all of the above?) and the rooms were comfortable and well equipped. My room had no wardrobe, but a curtain pole that swung across its width did a fine impersonation of one. This piece of equipment was more grand than the length of wire I'd had in Yanshu, but it was positioned a metre down from the ceiling and there was no way anyone less than a giant could have reached it. I hung my clothes on the cord that stretched from the wall fan instead, in the process disturbing a large spider that had come down from the ceiling to investigate me. My room also ran to a bed light, a rare commodity in Chinese hotels, which would have been fantastic if it had not been immovably fixed over the foot of the bed. If I got the urge to examine my toe nails in the middle of the night, however, I had a good light to do it by. The bottom halves of the floor-length curtains were covered with dark smears of polish that looked suspiciously like someone had cleaned their shoes on them. The plug of the television set had been smashed, apparently with a sledge-hammer, in order to remove its third prong and make it fit a two-point plug.

The communal bathrooms along the corridor were tatty and already bore much evidence of ill use. They contained a toilet, hand-basin and a hand held shower that ran directly onto the floor. There was no toilet paper; the maid dished you out a personal ration each day. The first bathroom I tried had no hot water, a fact that was only revealed to me after I had undressed and stood hopefully shivering on the tiled floor for some time. The wooden doors of the bathrooms were beginning to disintegrate from all the watering they received and the shower taps were falling off the walls. The bracket meant to hold the shower-head had been, as usual, the first casualty and washing was once again a one-handed affair. But it was most convenient that the lid of the toilet cistern was also missing. I could put the shower down in there while I soaped up.

My room ran to the luxury of a phone, but making calls presented the usual problems, and if I did not unplug it every night I was repeatedly disturbed by wrong numbers. No matter how often I explained to the switchboard operators that the call was not for me, they kept on ringing. I tried several times to call CITS, thinking that I could ask about the ship that was alleged to sail from Guangzhou to the north of Vietnam. But none of the staff who answered spoke English. When they couldn't understand me, they either hung up or put the phone down and walked away, hoping that I'd get tired of waiting and do the hanging up – thereby relieving them of doing so. I kept trying until I found someone who said, 'No such thing as a boat to Vietnam.' He gave me a number to call to enquire about a visa for Vietnam, but unfortunately this turned out to be an office for Chinese visa extensions. Persevering with the telephone, I eventually obtained the number of the Vietnamese Embassy and, after being hung up on many times, someone gave me the address, but only the street, not the number of the building. When I did finally locate the Vietnamese Embassy I discovered that the only way to find it was to have a map and the only way to obtain a map was – you guessed it – to go to the embassy.

The epic voyage of discovery to the embassy took two hours. Having taxied a long way across town, I was deposited in the street I had been given as their address. Simple, I thought, you walk up the street and find a sign that announces – Vietnamese Embassy. Wrong! The street ran for kilometre after kilometre and meandered all over the place. I walked and walked and then it started to rain. Deciding to call for more details, I stopped at a tiny grocery shop that had a red pay phone. I showed my map to the proprietor and he said, Yes, this was the street I wanted. I pointed to Vietnam in the phrase-book and this kind man obligingly found me the telephone code for Vietnam. I might as well have called Hanoi. Someone there may have had more idea of the whereabouts of the embassy in Guangzhou than the people who worked in it. They could not tell me how to get there, or the number of the building. The shopkeeper spoke to them. But they could not tell him either. The discussion continued to no avail, until the woman at the embassy put someone else on the line. He said, 'You wait there. I will come and get you.' I said, 'Are you one of the staff?' To which he replied, 'No, I am only here trying to get a visa for Vietnam too.' The shopkeeper took the phone and in great detail told this person how to find me. My would-be rescuer then said, 'You wait three minutes.' I waited thirteen and, deciding that my help was also lost, I set off again in the direction that I thought the embassy staff had been indicating. The shopkeeper didn't want me to leave. He worried that I might get lost again. We discussed this in pantomime and I finally convinced him that I would meet the man from the embassy on the way.

After walking a long way I came to the intersection of two main thoroughfares where a board with a large map of the city stood on the footpath. I was studying this map when a man rushed up to me and said, 'Excuse me. Are you the person who was ringing the embassy?' My saviour had found me! 'I've been looking everywhere for you,' he said. He told me that his name was Li and that he was an Australian Vietnamese who had lived in Sydney for twenty years. He had been selling veterinary supplies in China and now was trying to get a visa to do business in Vietnam. Even though he was Vietnamese by birth, it was still not easy for him to enter the country.

Li marched me kilometres further along the street, up a back lane, through an apartment building, out the other side and there it was, Guangzhou's best kept secret, the Vietnamese Embassy. My new friend took me inside the building and presented me proudly. 'Look! I have found her.' He should have been given a medal. I shook his hand with fervour, thinking that if this was an example of Vietnamese behaviour I couldn't wait to get there.

At the embassy a young woman officer dealt with me graciously but firmly. I asked if I could cross the border at the place named in the guide book as a possibility, but she said, 'The Mon Cai Pass will be a better place for you to cross. I will put this on your visa and then I can only let you go through that pass. And I can only let you go for a month.' I forked over sixty-five American dollars, a steep price for a visa, filled out numerous forms and was told to return in five days.

Leaving the embassy I found myself in one of Guangzhou's main drags, a huge dual highway with wide bike lanes and multitudes of trees on each side. Lock-up bicycle stations were everywhere. They were guarded by the Bike Police, some of whom even had guns in holsters on their hips. The Bike Police will take good care of your treadley machine, but woe betide you if you don't put it in the proper place. The delinquent bike will be towed away and impounded and a stiff ransom will be required to liberate it. Naturally the fine is especially hefty for foreigners.

Although Beijing has more cultural sights, I thought that Guangzhou's main streets were much nicer and, except at peak hour traffic times, not as crowded. I found the Friendship shop. It stocked everything except the one thing

I needed, deodorant. The person who can convince Chinese women that they smell will make a fortune! Someone had obviously persuaded them that they all had dirty teeth, and now after years of managing without western toothpaste and brushes, they have gone the whole hog and you could, for more than a hundred dollars, buy a teeth-whitening kit.

In the street I passed a white wedding with all the trimmings. Mao must have been doing cart-wheels in his mausoleum. A haunting bird call that I always associate with the tropics attracted my attention. Outside a shop a large bird, far from his habitat, squatted dismally on the floor of a cage so cruelly small that he could not even stretch his wings.

The next day I saw a far sadder thing. In front of a restaurant, live food – snakes, birds, chooks and animals – waited in wire cages to be selected for a meal. In one cage, too small for him to have stood up in, a handsome badger with a broad stripe down his nose, lay with his head on his paws. The day was warm, the cage was in the sun and there was no water. The badger looked up at me with lovely knowing eyes that were as intelligent as a sheep dog's. I felt so strongly for him that I nearly went in and bought him. But the real tragedy was that five days later I went past again and, to my dismay, he was still there. A little flatter on the wire mesh floor of his enclosure, he was a picture of abject misery. I stood, stunned with pity, before him. A big dead rat now kept the badger company in the cage. It was the lucky one.

The next day I woke to find that it was raining again and it poured off and on all day. Brolly aloft, I went for a walk around Shamian Island. It was a delightful place. I could have stayed there indefinitely. It was pleasant to stroll along the quiet, narrow streets that were more like private lanes. You could also take an enjoyable walk under leafy trees along the riverside, resting now and then on the seats provided at intervals. Once I spent hours stuck in a taxi in peak hour trying to cross the bridge to the island, and from then on I walked back from town along this path.

I noticed that in Guangzhou an attempt was made to remove rubbish from the river. A cleaning boat chugged regularly up and down while a worker scoured debris from the surface of the water with a scoop net on a pole. Among the craft that crowded the water, ferries criss-crossed the river ceaselessly. Where the ferries pulled into the bank a great flood of people, many wheeling bicycles, streamed ashore and swarmed all over the road. At these spots enterprising vendors sold hot chestnuts and other tempting edibles.

The Shamian Island area had all I needed, big hotels that were handy for the use of their post offices, coffee shops and other facilities, as well as plenty of cafés and restaurants to restore the inner man. One restaurant displayed a large cage of big writhing snakes at its front entrance. I gave it a miss. I'd done my snake eating act once and had no wish to repeat it. At the Victory Hotel the doorman helped me to park my brolly in the umbrella station. He locked its handle in a slot with a key that I kept until I returned to claim my umbrella. I discovered that you had to be wary of some of the staff at big hotels. The postal clerk at the Victory quoted me thirty yuan to send a postcard. I went to the other end of the counter where the receptionist asked me for five – at the post office the price was two and a half yuan.

Walking along the riverside I passed people, mostly old men, who sat watching life on the water, did their exercises or aired their birds – and I don't mean girlfriends. Shamian Island has two large parks that require a fee to enter. By now I understood how the infamous sign, 'No dogs or Chinese allowed' came about in Shanghai. Nothing has changed. The sign now says, 'Admission price' but it serves the same purpose – keeping out the Great Chinese

Unwashed, who otherwise would have stampeded into the park and demolished it – spitting, littering and sleeping in it overnight. The Chinese are just as class conscious, if not more so, than the British. For a supposedly classless society, China is more conscious of it than any place I have been.

At the bigger park on the riverbank, I paid one yuan to enter. The Chinese paid one tenth of a fan. But the park was worth my eight cents. Under the shelter of huge trees, it was beautifully kept. There were shrubs, palms, creepers, bushes, flowers, lawns and vantage points where you could sit and observe the river. The Chinese opera company, complete with full orchestral backing, were rehearsing in the rotunda at the water's edge. What an awful din.

For a while I joined an audience that surrounded a group of old men who were playing chess. Nearby a bunch of men and women clicked and clattered their bamboo mah jong pieces. This was very serious stuff; they had even brought a black cloth to cover the round stone table. Other park users did tai chi, read the paper, played cards, or had brought their birds in wicker cages for a walk.

The hostel café was attractive, but it cost a minimum of three yuan just to sit there, so I don't think they did much trade. I saw few people except the staff patronise it. And they used it as if they owned it. The guests seemed to be the last consideration of anything run by the government. We were just a nuisance to be tolerated, but not necessarily with kindness or good grace. We were secondary to the fact that the entire operation was there to provide the staff with work or, should I say, a place of employment. An example of this was the tremendous uproar the night shift commonly made in hotels. With absolutely no thought for those trying to sleep, they shouted, shrieked, yelled, telephoned, laughed, played music loudly, hawked and spat and turned the television on full bore. Their friends visited them and did the same. Viewing the hotel as their home, they acted accordingly. At the hostel I was woken several times every night by staff noise in the corridors, or at the attendant's station. And before dawn every morning I was roused by the Chinese man across the way screaming into his phone. Even through my ear plugs I could hear his long and convoluted conversations.

Instead of using the hostel café I frequented the one across the road. It had an English menu that offered a fifty per cent 'quicken charge' as well as squid beards, the mysteries of which I would like to have unravelled but never did. The menu's English subtitles were so scrambled that they were almost incomprehensible gibberish, and I could not decipher most of them. Once I tried to order fried eggs and dumplings but could not make myself understood. Finally the waitress pointed to a pile of fried eggs and sliced tinned ham that sat in a big enamel basin under the glass counter. I agreed and was served two eggs and some slices of ham – stone motherless cold straight from the bowl. Eating them with the chopsticks provided was a difficult operation. I had nothing with which to cut the food and it is not easy to get a great slice of solid ham into your face with any degree of delicacy without somehow reducing its size. I also ordered 'French toast'. This strange item arrived after I had finished the Battle of the Ham. It was an inch thick doorstop of bread that had had something unidentifiable spread on it and then been fried in a sweet oil.

One day while I was having lunch in the café I kept hearing strange noises that I presumed must be coming from a child. Then I realised that a woman eating at one of the tables had a live chook dangling upside down off the edge of her handbag. Later as I passed around the back of the café I saw her delivering it to the kitchen door. You couldn't say that the food there was not fresh.

Through the window of my room in the hostel I could hear the hoot of boats on the river, and I looked out onto several blocks of flats across the way. The apartments had no blinds or curtains and through their windows and balcony doors I could clearly see the residents going about their lives. Although the flats looked fairly upmarket, they only ran to two rooms plus ablutions and, judging from the way washing was hung out on the mesh-enclosed balconies a few pieces at a time daily, they had no washing machines. Several caged birds were also hung out on balconies during the day and I could hear them twittering away among the pot plants, while in the evenings I listened to someone practising the piano.

Across the road from the hostel the White Swan Hotel, the ultimate in magnificent opulence, fronted onto the Pearl River. I visited the hotel to sample its loos and use its other salubrious facilities. It covered hectares of ground and a ramble around it left me almost exhausted. The White Swan boasted several massive foyers with incredible decors. One was dominated by a jade boat as big as a house, while in the main foyer a waterfall cascaded into a large pond that contained even larger goldfish and a huge jade carving of a mountain covered with flowers. Here I said hello to a batch of fellow-Australians – a flock of multi-coloured budgerigars in a very large gilded cage. As I wandered about, every now and then I came upon long rosewood benches on which magnificent bonsai pots containing tiny, but ancient, trees stood. There were also heaps of very expensive shops offering the ultimate in luxury goods. An American guest told me that upstairs the rooms were pretty ordinary, however, and the usual things failed to work. Learning that the White Swan had a medical clinic and a resident doctor, I decided to ask for some anti-malarial tablets. A fat lot of use that was. The doctor did not understand one word I said, even with the help of the phrasebook. I thought this curious. The people in the street did better than that. The doctor apparently did not have a clue what I meant by anti-malarial. So I tried the hotel's fantastic big chemist shop. The staff there had never heard of the stuff either. I began to feel that I was the strange one, asking for this exotic product, yet malaria is prevalent in South China and causes many deaths. I had used my supply of anti-malarial tablets travelling through Indonesia and hadn't planned to be anywhere that I would need more.

Later I visited a couple of the large pharmacies in the town. You could tell from the goods they stocked that the Chinese are a nation of hypochondriacs, who widely practise DIY medicine. It was possible to buy everything imaginable over the counter, as well as instruments for home surgery and dental work. You could even buy boxes of teeth to make up your own set of falsies, or to whack in a spare or two. But I found no malaria prophylaxis or treatment. The pharmacists did not even know the word 'malaria', despite my now having it written in Chinese on a piece of paper. But I was offered potions, pills and antibiotics enough to cure the ails of the world as well as any stray headache, diarrhoea, sore throat or toothache I might suffer.

Then, during my investigations of the small Shamian Island streets, I spied a building with a small red cross painted on its wall. On internal inspection this place turned out to be a local medical clinic, although it appeared to have once been a warehouse. Stepping in off the street I found a large hall that contained two antique wooden counters topped by iron grills and bars. I looked through these and saw what resembled an old counting house on the other side where a man in a white coat sat at a dilapidated wooden table that pretended to be a desk. His outfit was crowned by a theatre cap. Ready to do instant surgery on me? This impressive gentleman could not understand what I wanted, but he was exceedingly polite and, signalling that I should wait, sent for help. The reinforcements arrived – a young couple in army uniform who spoke English. They told me that I should go to the Foreigner's Clinic which was located in one of the big hospitals. Then they obligingly wrote its phone number and address in Chinese for me.

I took a taxi to the hospital. Another agreeable surprise, it was a marvellous place. It had large grounds full of gardens with pretty plants and lofty trees full of singing birds. It seemed more like a delightful park than an institution. The hospital wards were arranged along colonnaded and covered walkways that now and then passed under pagoda-shaped arches and were lined with shaded seats. And it was all kept squeaky clean by small women who were busy on the ends of very large brooms. Proceeding along a walkway, I looked in some of the windows and concluded that, although it may have had wonderful grounds, the hospital's medical care looked primitive. Theatre patients returning from their operations were trundled past me on the walkway. The unconscious patients were jolted along on trolleys wheeled by orderlies. Although they were accompanied by a legion of their relatives and onlookers, who shared the duty of holding up the drip bottle (the trolleys were too ancient to run to the luxury of a drip stand), there was no medical help in attendance. It all seemed very casual.

Now and then I saw a sign written in Pinyin, but nothing like a Foreigners' Clinic. I asked some staff I encountered, but they just turned their backs and giggled. I kept asking more people and was pointed upstairs. On the third floor of the building, I found a surfeit of nurses, six of whom lounged idly in an office. They giggled uncontrollably at the mere sight of me and when I spoke to them went into hysterics. But I persevered and eventually they tried to find someone who could speak to me. The nurses wore old-fashioned, clean, but unironed, white cotton uniforms that reached almost to their ankles, had sleeves down to their wrists, collars up to their chins and trousers underneath them. Their feet were clad in any white shoes they could find, even very unprofessional looking high heels. The odd one wore a cap.

Then a very superior and supercilious young man with a white coat and a very bad cast in one eye, materialised and proceeded to tell me off. He berated me soundly for being in the wrong place. When he paused for breath I said, 'Now look here. I can't help it if I am in the wrong place. I am only asking directions.' At this he calmed down and drew me a mud map and in the end we parted friends.

Even with the aid of the map I still couldn't find the Foreigners' Clinic. I did find the enormous outpatient and casualty department, but by now this was closed to business for the usual long lunch. A few hopeful patients seated on the benches that lined the walls gawked at me as I wandered around. I could have done what I liked, there was no one to stop me.

Finally I came across a woman in uniform who ambled by clutching a large white enamel bowl slopping over with bloody water. I followed this Chinese Florence Nightingale to a desk where a bevy of nurses promptly went into convulsions of laughter at my appearance. In the fullness of time, however, one of them recovered sufficiently to call a porter and put me in his charge saying, 'You go.' I went. Back again to where I had started. The porter and I came to a building which sported an English sign – Department of Gerontology! My guide led me into the first Geriatric Clinic I have had the misfortune to visit as a patient – I admit that the first bloom of youth has long since fled my cheek, but I don't think I qualify for aged care just yet. At the far end of the Geriatric waiting room we came to a sign that announced – Foreigners' Clinic. So there was one all the time! It was just that almost no one in the hospital knew about it.

The Foreigners' Clinic was empty. The porter knocked on a door and opening it revealed a nurse laid out on an examination couch having her siesta. He shook her awake. No feeble cries for help from a distressed patient would summon these stalwart ministering angels. The nurse opened the door of an adjoining room to disclose a very large, very handsome, male doctor – also asleep on a couch. He was not thrilled to see me. He quickly found a female doctor to take over. I wished I could explain that I did not mean to disturb them and would gladly wait until they were sufficiently refreshed by sleep. Handsome returned to his slumbers and the ladies – I had four in attendance by this time – did not say, 'Wait until opening time,' but with incredible patience, and no English, tried to find out what I wanted. I drew diagrams. I performed pantomime. I did charades. We consulted the pharmacopoeia together and they eventually worked out what I was asking for. Then they told me that they did not have it! They said to wait twenty minutes more and they would get their superior.

While I waited I had ample time to examine the clinic. It was a spotlessly clean time capsule from the 1940s. Instruments and thermometers rested on layers of cotton wool in glass jars half-filled with sterilising fluid, wooden-framed screens leaned against the walls and metal stands held enamelled basins. There were shelves and cupboards of white painted wood and plastic flowers.

The superior arrived. A gracious woman with a little English, she told me she might have something to offer me. After a lot of time spent writing notes and sending messages to people – the phones didn't seem to work – she produced some literature on the drug in question for me to read. I agreed to try it and was handed over to a nurse who took me to the pharmacy where I sat on a wooden form in a long corridor until I was called to the counter and asked to contribute. The consultation had only cost a few cents for all that work, but for the exotic and rare pills, reeling with shock, I had to cough up sixty dollars.

Outside once more I realised that the process of procuring the pills had taken two and a half hours. I taxied to the bank to restock my funds. Afterwards I caught sight of a Muck Donalds in the distance and was making a bee line for it at a hard trot when I passed a group on the footpath. Sprawled beside a wall on the busy street, with their few tattered belongings around them, were a dirty and ragged youngish man and two male children. The man held the smaller child across his knees. It seemed to be asleep, but it looked sick. He stroked its face gently, tenderly, and looked at it with such love in his eyes that I was moved. The other child lay alongside him on the ground. They looked exhausted, as though they had come far and suffered greatly to do so. They were not begging. They just sat there while all the world went by unheeding. And me with them.

At Mac Maggot's bright beckoning entrance it hit me that I had felt the same misery in them as I had in the badger. I walked up to the counter, money in hand, looked at the pictures of the food on the wall with the image of the sick child behind my eyes and lost my appetite. I couldn't help the badger, but I could help him. I turned around, went back and kneeling on the ground laid the money beside the child's hand.

Since I had arrived in Guangzhou several days before, the weather had been cool, raining or overcast, but then a lovely spring-like day dawned. Soon children accompanied by their minders were enjoying the sunshine in Shamian Island's pretty street gardens. I watched them playing as I waited for my lunch at the tiny table of a sidewalk café. I loved this café. A tree grew right through its centre and out of the roof. I remembered how the foyer of the hospital I had visited had also been built around a massive tree. A high glass atrium accommodated it all – branches, top, the lot. And another tree trunk went through the middle of the outpatient's waiting room. Despite the fact that China is not very friendly to the environment, other countries could learn from the way they sometimes refuse to cut down trees.

A young man near me at the café sipped a can of Carlsberg beer elegantly through a straw and a strong smell of petrol wafted over from the gutter where the cook and his assistant – identified by their high chef's hats and white aprons – laboured away trying to start the generator with a pull rope. They both wore knee-high gum boots which gave me pause to wonder how mucky it got in their kitchen.

After lunch I walked across the bridge to the local market. It covered a lot of ground, flowing up and down covered alleys so narrow that there was only enough space to squeeze between the stalls. I struggled quickly through the reeking meat section at the entrance. Thankfully this soon gave way to the wonderful smell of herbs. They were sold dried or naturally fresh in strands or bundles. I had no idea what most of them were, but I recognised camomile. Woven into round fragrant mats, it was ready to make into tea or to blonde your hair.

I stepped back repulsed when a vendor held out two bear paws with great claws attached. Bear paws are considered a gastronomic delicacy. Not for me, though. The medicines included dried lizards flattened into the shape of the emperor's fan and dried, coiled snakes, repulsive and real-looking. And anything that resembled a phallus was sold as a 'tonic' – a euphemism for an aphrodisiac.

In the fresh food department, I saw cages of live birds of all kinds as well as dogs, turtles, lizards and snakes. Remembering how Saint Patrick had needed to perform a miracle to clear the snakes out of Ireland, I thought that the job should have been given to the Chinese. They'd have done it quicker – they would have eaten them out. Moving on, I bought a string of fresh water pearls for a ridiculously low price and had a new strap fitted to my watch at a watchmaker's tiny stand. Once again I unwittingly examined the contraceptives. The packets always look so inviting that they get me in every time. Then I saw numerous stalls lined with row after row of bras. Something about them seemed weird so I administered the prod test. My finger encountered a rock solid substance. Now I knew why the girls in China did not look flat chested. But wearing a bra like that must feel as though a couple of saucepan lids have been strapped to your chest.

After twisting and turning through the market streets, I found myself in the kind of small back lanes that I enjoy. This was where the Chinese people lived, shopped and worked. I especially liked the roof-tops of the crowded and narrow houses. Some were pretty and decorated with gardens and fancy balustrades; others looked as though they were about to fall off, or crumble at any minute. On many balconies piles of junk, makeshift lean-tos and the odd tree in a pot were pushed together, surrounded by any kind of fencing that could be called into use as a barricade to stop it all falling down.

Through the hostel's resident travel agent I learned that the nearest big town to the border into Vietnam was Nanning. I could travel to Wuzhou, which was part of the way there on the Pearl River by boat and from there boats left for Nanning. A riverboat departed from Guangzhou on the evening of the day my Vietnamese visa had been promised, so I bought a ticket. I half-expected not to be granted the visa, but it was duly handed over to me by a young Vietnamese lady in a beautiful embroidered blouse. Once again I was told that I was only permitted to cross the border at the Mon Cai Pass and only on the date set down on my visa. I was still unsure of the location, which I could not find on my map, but I thought that it was in the mountains.

The day of the boat's departure was again lovely, birds were singing and the sun shone brightly. I filled in the time until boarding by sitting in the park, then I did the rounds of the posh hotel lobbies in the vicinity. Some of them were tourist attractions themselves and in them I could indulge in one of my hobbies – people watching. It surprised me that hotel staff never threw me out of these places. It must have been because of my white face. It came in handy sometimes.

Boarding the boat was easy. A helpful member of the wharf staff pointed the way and I went relatively placidly onto the vessel. There was not a big crowd of passengers and there were smooth ramps I could roll my wheeled luggage down. But the boat was so small that at first I thought it was a day-tripper. It had only two decks and a cargo hold below. Immediately I stepped over the gang-plank and onto the deck, however, I was hit by the stench of the toilets. It was not a happy welcome.

My first glimpse of the ship was not appealing. It was old, tatty and worn and a row of fire buckets were once again the sum total of the emergency equipment. There were only a few cabins and they were grouped around an open central area, forward on the first deck. All one end of the deck above was taken up by a single large communal cabin that contained two tiers of boards with rush mats spread on them edge to edge, on which people were laid out in two long rows like peas in a pod.

I stood on deck in the prow to watch our departure. Suddenly a bellowing, 'Hellooooo' came from somewhere above. I jumped a foot in the air and, turning, saw the captain above me on the bridge with a megaphone in his hand and his face split in a watermelon sized grin that displayed lots of teeth. 'Hello,' I shouted back. 'How are you?' he roared and laughing loudly blew a tremendous blast on the horn. I almost fell overboard. 'I was fine before that!' I bawled back. He roared with laughter again and we left.

The boat edged away from the dockside, swung out into midstream and turning downriver, set off at a good pace into the setting sun with the flow of the stream. A peasant in a faded blue cotton jacket and rope sandals crept up to watch me silently, open mouthed with awe. I tried not to do anything too interesting, shocking or entertaining, but I still held him in thrall. 'Dabidaze' – 'big nose' he finally whispered.

When dark fell half an hour later, we were still plying through Guangzhou. We passed many barges loaded with building materials that were so low in the water it amazed me that they didn't sink. Some actually had water washing over their freeboard. We sailed past the White Swan Hotel, festooned with lights like a fantastic Christmas tree, and on the outskirts of the city, row after row of factories.

My cabin was very small. It contained two wooden bunks covered with rush mats. There were no mattresses or sheets, but there was a doona and a tiny pillow. The ever-present thermos and cups sat in a plastic holder on a small wooden desk.

I located the dining room on the top deck. It was a wonder and beat the eating establishment of any other boat I had been on in China. Comfortable and well equipped with real tables and chairs, it also had windows with curtains and wall and ceiling lights, almost all of which had most bulbs working – a major achievement. There had even been a cheery attempt to brighten it up with decorations. The staff were helpful and I managed to get some food by the Look and Point method. Even the food was great. I ate the best mushrooms I have tasted since I collected them myself in farm paddocks, along with great big clumps of a green vegetable that looked like celery. I had no implements to cut the greens, so I had to shove what I could in my mouth, bite off what was left hanging out, and chomp. Very elegant. A man who spoke a few words of English and his girlfriend shared my table. They were friendly, but he smoked non-stop.

The boat did not run to a sitting room, but after dinner a

television was set up in the open space between the cabins and I was invited to watch a film. A micro-sized shop near the dining room sold life-sustaining necessities such as cigarettes, noodles, biscuits and booze, and Chinese music invaded my ears wherever I went.

Some time after dark we stopped in mid-stream, hooted three times and a big sampan pulled out from the shore to land a dozen or so people on board our boat. From then on we stopped and hooted at intervals and each time we did passengers or goods came out to us. This operation woke me at about two in the morning and I looked out of my porthole. By the silvery light of an almost full moon I saw the river, its surface dotted here and there with the soft lights of small boats, unfolding gently between the outline of low hills.

In the morning I could see that the riverside was ter-raced with rice paddies and that the hills were separated by veils of mist that lay low between their folds. Soon mist also started to roll off the river until everything was obscured and we were creeping along through a world of dense fog.

When the fog lifted later, I saw an occasional village or town. Clusters of wooden boats nuzzled the shore at their feet; their lives were obviously dominated by the river. The Pearl River was calm and nowhere near as wide as the Yangtze, but the villages were all perched halfway up hill-sides – an indication that flooding was common. And land-slides must have been too. I saw a place where an entire cliff of red earth had plunged into the river. Further on, the hills became heavily wooded and barges with big loads of logs went past downstream.

The boat's ablution block was unisex. To wash my face and clean my teeth I had to join a medley of men and women who were busy splashing in a row of wash-basins that lined the wall. The toilets were a hole in the tiled floor, but at least they were not communal. Each small cubby hole had a half-sized swing door.

We reached Wuzhou, a large town built high on the river-bank, at a quarter to twelve the next day. I was now back in Guangxi province. When I got off the boat I hired a quiet boy who picked up my bag and calmly took charge of me. At the top of the inevitable thousand steps, he took me to the ticket office and tried to help me to get a ticket to Nanning. It proved unavailable. The river level was too low at this time for passenger boats to navigate any further upriver, so he took me to the bus depot instead. Then he told me which hotel to go to and put me in a taxi, getting out my map and making sure the lady driver understood where I wanted to go. Despite all this extra attention, he did not ask me for more than the price we had agreed on to get up the steps, but I gave him a bonus. The people of Wuzhou seemed friendly. When I had consulted my phrasebook in the street I had drawn an instant audience and two female students emerged from the crowd and accompanied me and my helper to the bus ticket office. Here all my entourage and an obliging woman official joined forces to ensure that I got the best bus.

The hotel the taxi took me to was almost opposite the boat dock. An old four-storeyed building, it had terrazzo floors and a wide marble staircase. Some hotel receptionists hadn't even looked at my visa, but this one took what seemed to be forever scrutinising and deciphering it. I was given a room on the top floor. There was no lift. But it was good for my legs! When I was told that the room cost only eight dollars, I expected a grubby slum. Amazingly I found a small, spotless single room with an alcove at one end that housed a tiny but clean bathroom. The hand basin even looked as though it had been introduced to the Ajax. A large galvanised-iron bucket that appeared to be the clothes washing facility reposed in one corner and a cumbersome wooden toilet seat hung from a nail on the wall. There was also the usual hand-shower with the usual broken wall bracket from which, I had been told, hot water only flowed after seven in the evening.

The floor of my room was covered with check-patterned tiles which gave away its secret past; it had formerly been part of an old verandah. The mosquito net coiled over the bed reminded me that I was in malaria country again, but I could not fathom why the ceiling fan over the bed had neat newspaper parcels wrapped around its blades.

From the barred window in the alcove I looked down on the flat roofs and tiny upstairs back porches of the surrounding houses. A couple of the roofs had veggies growing in mini plots of earth. I heard a cat crying and searched for it apprehensively, fearing that it might be tonight's tea at the restaurant below. Instead I discovered a big white moggie rubbing the legs of a woman who was tending a plot of vegetables. He was telling her that it was time for his dinner. Meanwhile, on an adjacent balcony, a small boy kung-fued a cushion that had been tied on a washing line and a man performed his ablutions in a tin bowl.

In the restaurant attached to the hotel I was the only patron, but I was not alone. Eight staff gossiped loudly at a nearby table. After much reference to the phrasebook, one girl more enterprising than the rest brought forth a menu that had some English translations. I ordered what I thought was mixed vegetables but only received a huge plate of the green vegetable dish I had had on the boat. It looked like the weed I saw men dredging up from the river, but I seriously hoped it was not. Not after what could be seen floating in those waters.

My dinner contained masses of garlic. I ate at least a dozen cloves with never a thought for my poor fellow travellers who were about to be incarcerated for twelve hours in a bus with me the next day.

In the evening I went walking for a couple of hours. The riverside wharves contained extensive covered markets and a busy night market also spread through the small back streets close to the river. Everyone seemed to be out shopping or strolling. I bought some of the many varieties of fruit that were plentiful here and, as I had started to feel a bit squiffy since eating my dinner, I bought a big bottle of pickled chilli to take as a prophylactic. No bug can survive in your stomach if you drown it in chilli.

Returning to my room I had a wonderful hot shower and went to bed. The old iron bed springs creaked and the lumpy coils prodded me, but I slept soundly off and on despite the noise the staff made outside my door all night.

8 Big Nose in Nanning

By nine o'clock in the morning I had transported myself to the comfortable Wuzhou bus station down by the river. When it was time to go, I tramped down a flight of stairs to the waiting bus. It was neither deluxe nor airconditioned, as I had been promised, but it was a big improvement on the standard of comfort provided by some of the other local buses. My bags were heaved up in front with the driver, who was hemmed in with luggage by the time we left.

At the scheduled departure time and with the bus only three-quarters full, we set off. I thought this was great, but I cheered too soon. We drove two doors further down the street and pulled into the rear of another bus depot where fifteen immense rolls of carpet, various large boxes, bundles and baggage and five passengers, complete with their breakfast and several bottles of Chinese whisky, waited. This band of hopefuls looked as though they had every intention of getting all their cargo, as well as themselves aboard. Weighty discussions with the driver ensued. Eventually he dismounted and, going to the rear of the bus, opened a small freight door that gave access to the row of seats across the back. Then, with an extraordinary amount of shouting from everybody concerned and about forty five thousand spectators, the driver and passengers pushed the stuff in. Sweating and straining they man-handled some of the rolls of carpet across the back seats, stacking them up to the roof and obliterating any chance the driver had of seeing out of the rear window. Each roll required a preamble of five minutes of shouting and screaming before it was stowed. When all but six rolls of carpet were finally aboard, I thought, Well done! But they hadn't finished, not by a long shot. They dragged the rest to the front of the bus, hauled it in and filled the aisle. Then they put the bags and bundles on top. Lastly the passengers clambered up. Three of them sat on top of the mountain in the middle of the aisle; the other two got down on the only half square metre of floor left vacant and had a picnic with their breakfast noodles and bottles of spirit. They seemed quite unperturbed that this procedure had taken forty minutes and we were now running late.

It took another hour to leave Wuzhou behind. At first we drove along cliffs that looked down into the river, then we were on tortuous country roads among the now familiar terraces of rice paddies. Even though there was no sun and a greyish-blue haze of pollution persisted the countryside was attractive. The peridot green of rice in the foreground, behind it sugar cane, with its lovely apple green stalks and bamboo-like flutey spikes, and in the background the blue mountains.

The bus progressed slowly, still collecting passengers. I should have known better than to think that this would not happen just because I was on a classier sort of bus. When all the seats were filled, people sat on top of the carpet in the aisles; one girl leaned her head on the seat of the man in front of her and almost pushed him off it. He moved over to accommodate her. Another carpet dweller practically sat on top of the bloke in the seat in front of him. But no one seemed to think this behaviour was objectionable.

At least on this bus trip the group of men who sat around me did not smoke. In fact, they kept opening windows and telling the smokers off! Apart from the young doctor I had met on the ship from Dalian, they were the first Chinese men I had encountered who did not smoke. Sitting next to me was a middle-aged man who wore glasses with lenses as thick as the bottoms of Coke bottles. We had a limited conversation in which he told me that he and his two companions, a young man and woman, were teachers. He asked if I was one too. I hoped this was because I looked intelligent.

We stopped for lunch at a small wayside place where the locals were greatly intrigued by me. There were only two other women on the bus, and I kept a watchful eye on them, following them wherever they went in the hope that I might be led to a loo. Finally I hit the jackpot. The women went down some stairs that went underneath the roadhouse.

As I descended the stairs I was delighted to see a row of five big pink faces look up at me, while ten bright, beady eyes drank me in with unblinking fascination. They belonged to beautiful young adult pigs as fat as butter, with healthy pointed ears and lively stupid grins. The pigs were housed under the same roof and very close to the family's sleeping quarters, but in a spot with much more light. I am very fond of pigs. Breeding them and keeping them as pets changed my misconceptions about them. I now know that they are intelligent, clean, loving and affectionate. It made my day to see those cheery little souls.

Later this day our bus was halted by roadworks in a village where a street market was in progress. We stopped beside the meat section, and judging by the amount of trotters present, the meat was mostly pig. Slabs of bloody animal flesh, exposed and covered with multitudes of flies, lay directly on the wood of dirty old trestles and was being handled by passers-by. They picked it up, played with it, put it down and moved on.

Hours passed in the bus as we climbed gradually towards the mountains, I knitted, read and refrained from drinking too much. There had been one stop for relief a few hours after lunch. The driver pulled the bus up beside a field of sugar cane and all the men dashed into it. There was no way I was joining them. Not only for reasons of decorum – it *was* broad daylight – but also because sugar cane is a notorious harbourer of vermin and I had just read that millions of reptiles resided at the snake farm near Wuzhou. One million a year are sent from there to the tables of restaurants all over China, Hong Kong and Macau. Working out that they had to get those snakes from somewhere around here, I decided that there was no way I was putting my bottom anywhere near the ground in this district. I let the men have the sugar cane all to themselves.

The bus was equipped with a video machine, but thankfully we were not subjected to the usual Kung Fu film. Of all the unlikely items, we were shown an Asian beauty contest. The female contestants were dazzling, but they all looked the same, like clones of Joan Collins straight out of *Dynasty*. Like over-dressed Barbie dolls weighed down with masses of gaudy jewellery, with hair that resembled fairy floss that had been glued into solid shapes with litres of spray, and faces that were plastered with pounds of paint, they wore clothes that were pure soap opera; brilliant coloured shiny material bountifully covered with glitter. In the talent section, the contestants were brought forward to perform like monkeys. One danced the tango, one sang and one did a bit of karate. It was the sort of degrading affair that feminists condemn, and in this case I would have agreed with them.

I imagined that we would stop for another meal towards evening, but as it began to get dark we started climbing very steep hills and there was no village in sight. The bus ground on, up and up, passing other broken down or overturned buses along the way. We had almost reached the top of the mountain chain and I was congratulating myself on choosing a superior sort of bus, when a tremendous, clattering crash reverberated underneath us. It sounded as though something very big had fallen off the bus. We stopped and after half an hour of much shouting and carrying on with flash-lights, the driver climbed back in and we started off again very slowly. Now we had no head-lights and in total darkness we were descending downhill extremely steeply, with the driver braking often as if he could not see what was ahead. I prayed fervently that what had fallen off the bus was in no way connected with the brakes or steering. Careering along in this uncertain, but precipitous manner, we zoomed down a long way, until we came to one of the many toll gates that were found on these roads. Here we shuddered to a final sickening halt. With the help of all the available men, the bus was pushed to the side of the road, and we were left sitting there in the frigid black of night.

After about an hour, a small local bus came along. My schoolteacher friend went out to look at it and came back indicating that I should go with him. I had no idea where, but it was now raining heavily and anything seemed better than spending the night on a mountainside in the freezing cold. Half of the other bus passengers got up and left, so I followed. My friend had saved me a seat in the new bus and I was poised in mid-air, with one foot on the step, when a man shoved me aside and knocked me over. I went down in the mud, in a tangle of bags. This man wasn't being intentionally rude, he just didn't think. When he heard me shriek as I fell to the ground, he turned around, dusted me off and helped me onto the bus. Then, to add insult to injury, a conductor arrived and made me pay another fare.

Bumping along towards Nanning at the thirty kilometres an hour that was the maximum speed this latest conveyance could muster, I had plenty of time to be grateful to it, bone-shaker though it was. Although it sounded like a sick chaff cutter, it was transport and it seemed to be going in the right direction. I looked out of the window but could see nothing. We were now on a small back road and outside there was only an inky void.

When we reached Nanning, I discovered that the teachers had decided to take me under their wing. Looking at my map, they agreed that the Airport Hotel I pointed to would be suitable. Ignoring my assurances that I would find it myself, they carried my bags to a taxi and the young woman came with me. At the hotel I tried to pay the taxi fare, but the girl, who was going to continue on in it, refused to take any money. I was absolutely floored by the kindness of these people.

The Airport Hotel was in the main street of town, but the name written in Pinyin outside it was not Airport, but CAAC. Another trap for travellers in China is that sometimes a guidebook will give you English translations that are not the same as the hotel's version of them. This hotel belonged to the notorious airline, but I did not hold that against it. From the street its façade was imposing, but the foyer strongly resembled a public lavatory. Once again the receptionist spent a long time examining my visa. It seemed difficult for her to understand the extension that had been added, or whether I was legally permitted to stay, but eventually she decided that I was.

I was directed to a room on the sixth floor. At least, so far, the lift was working. For a mere twenty dollars I had a room with everything my heart could desire, including plumbing leaks, and hot water from an instant electric heater. I even had a door that opened on to a long narrow balcony that ran the length of the building and was entirely caged in with iron bars so that no one could climb in or out. All the rooms had balconies, but I wondered for what purpose they had been intended. Their enclosing walls were too high to see out. Their only function that I could see was to house a washing line. But, as it was still spitting with rain, the covered balcony was a boon. Although I was dead tired I washed some clothes and went to bed feeling virtuous. It was great to hang my washing out in the open again.

My room had a wonderfully comfortable bed, the only decent pillow I had come across in China, lights that were in the right places and even a television that worked. I was supplied with numerous comforts such as shoe cleaner, soap and toothpaste, but no towel. And no key. I was still not that trustworthy. And bliss, the place was quiet at night. To make up for this lapse I was shocked awake at seven in the morning by some terrible shrieking. The propaganda machine was at work and the message was piped through a loudspeaker in the public square. In Nanning, however, perhaps to soften you up for the blow, it was always preceded by Beethoven's winsome 'Für Elise' played at top pitch.

In the dim light of a drizzly morning I looked over the wall of my balcony. Down below on one side I could see into the yard of a large bus station and on the other into the backs of tiny apartments. A grotty view.

As I walked out of the hotel I saw was a young girl of about twenty dressed in simple worker's clothes standing against a wall. A giant cardboard placard hung on a rope around her neck. It reached all the way down her body and out past her shoulders and was covered with Chinese characters. By her dejected look I guessed that she had done something wrong and this was her punishment. It made me feel sick to see her shamed in this cruel manner. When I first saw the unfortunate sinner, only a couple of people had stopped to look at her, but the second time a large crowd had gathered and one little old woman in a Mao suit was bent over in front of the girl reading every word of the placard aloud. I felt very sorry for her.

The Airport Hotel was conveniently central and I could walk to most places I wanted to visit. I had read that there was a train to Dhongxing, the village near the border crossing into Vietnam, so I went to the railway station first. It was at the far end of the main street and could be safely reached by a massive underground walkway which was filled with vendors' stalls. I thought this was a marvellous idea. You were provided with entertainment, as well as the definite advantage of getting across the square without being killed. Emerging from the underpass, I found myself at the foot of an extensive flight of steps that led up to the railway station. Here I was accosted by a mob of beggars who looked like gypsies. One woman pushed a little boy about three years old at me. I could see that he was a sweet child under the dirt. She said, '*Loala, loala*,' and seemed to be telling him to 'get the foreigner'. He seized hold of my pants and hung on desperately as though his life depended on it. I did not want to give money to the woman, but I was afraid the child might be punished if he was not successful. I saw more beggars in Nanning than I had elsewhere and I was frequently solicited for money. Apart from the people from ethnic minority groups who haunted the railway station most of the beggars were old people.

At the ticket-office some helpful workers, with the aid of the phrasebook, told me that no trains ran to or near the village of Dhongxing. They said there was a bus and took great pains to direct me to the bus station. For once I had no problem finding my way. I was living next door to it. If the phrasebook was right, the bus I needed left at three the afternoon after next.

Everyone I met in Nanning was helpful but highly amused at finding me there. They only see the odd foreigner. Nanning, a port on the Yu River, is the capital of the Guangxi Zhuang Autonomous Region and a stronghold of China's minority nationalities. The surrounding district is the home of many ethnic groups, including the Zhuang, Miao, Yao, and Yi, each of which has its own traditions, culture and costumes. Nanning means 'tranquillity of the south' and, located below the Tropic of Cancer, it is China's southernmost big city – although its streets felt more like a country town.

As I walked back along the main street, I came upon a small hotel that had a sign outside, 'Travel Toursit' it said. I went in out of curiosity. In the office, an obliging young lady gave me detailed information about crossing to Vietnam. I was thinking that CITS had certainly improved, when I discovered that this was not CITS but a private travel agency. The presiding angel turned out to be a charming Chinese-Vietnamese, who was dying to practise her English. We had a good chat and I found out far more about getting into Vietnam than I had been told at the Vietnamese Embassy. It was a great relief to discover that I was heading for the right place as I had still not been sure.

In the front window of the restaurant nearest my hotel, several cooked and glazed dogs hung enticingly by their noses. But I chose to eat at a café called the American Fried Chicken Company that had, despite its name, Chinese food. Here I had the only cup of percolated coffee I got in China, but I had to send it back three times to get it without milk and sugar. It came served in a big glass that was too hot to hold, but at least there was a lot of it. I drank it to the sound of chomping noises all around me – other patrons doing exactly what your mother trained you not to do on pain of death – eat with your mouth open.

It started to rain again and a profusion of purple mushrooms sprang up – plastic capes shaped to suit bicycle riders. Someone must have got a lot of purple plastic very cheaply; it was everywhere. As it rained for almost all of the three days I was in Nanning, I spent much of my time walking about in it. On one occasion two women stopped, stared at me and began to laugh riotously. I confronted them and asked them what was funny. They pointed good naturedly to my nose. I had become a spectator sport.

Across the road from the hotel I found a place that took only an hour to develop films. I even received a refund on a couple of prints that did not come out. As I had already paid for developing the film in advance I thought the assistant was asking me for extra money. I was about to hand over the sum she had written down when I discovered that she wanted to give it to me. The staff thought this was extremely comical and had a great laugh about it.

I was rejected by two taxi drivers whom I tried to persuade to drive me to the post office. They said they did not know what, or where, it was. When the third came along I didn't give her a chance to say no. I jumped into the front seat with her. Lots of sign language and use of the *Traveller's Bible* (Lonely Planet) resulted in my being deposited in front of the telephone exchange, not the post office. I walked a lot further looking for it and I eventually wandered into what I thought was a hotel to ask directions of an old man I could see inside. It was actually the police station. The elderly policeman walked me down the street and, at the corner, pointed the way and crossed his two forefingers. I decided that this meant either ten minutes or a cross road. It was neither, but I found the post office.

At midday the next day I checked out of the hotel, left my bags at the bus station and then discovered I was like an orphan in the snow. What do you do when it is raining, you are in a strange town and you don't have anywhere to go? The rain had steadily increased until it was too heavy to walk about in, there were no picture theatres, and the museum had shut for a three-hour lunch. I opted to sit in the bus station, which is always a good place for people watching. Here you see the real Chinese, who make up most of the bus travellers. Trains are too expensive for them. Several men came to stand in front of me and stare. They were dressed in rope sandals, straw hats and faded Mao suits that stopped a couple of inches short of their ankles and wrists, fashion guaranteed to make the wearer look a proper dork. Put a heart throb like Mel Gibson in a suit like that and even he'd look the same.

When I had bought my ticket to Dhongxing, the seller explained something to me. I had no idea what she said, although I was able to deduce that my bus left from post number seven in the station. Now that I was leaving China, I was finally able to decipher a few characters, including some numbers. But no one I asked seemed sure about which bus left for Dhongxing. Later I learned that this was because Dhongxing was not the destination of any of the buses – you had to change to another later on. I said, 'Dhongxing?' to the conductor of the bus standing by post seven. She looked uncertain, but assured me that the bus was the correct one for my ticket and to emphasise this threw my bags onto the bus for me. This was the only time an official person ever helped me on to a conveyance in China. I followed the bags onto the bus. More passengers arrived. They seemed to be asking the driver where he was going, so I asked him too, repeating like a parrot, 'Dhongxing, Dhongxing' my one word of communication, my passport. The driver didn't seem to know where he was going, but he had the nerve to sneer at me because I didn't.

An old man lumped two hessian bags aboard. I smiled at him and said, '*Neehow,*' and he told me – I think – that he was going to Dhongxing and I should watch him. 'Like a hawk, old son,' I replied. Although the bus waited for a long time while the conductor tried to drum up more trade, six people were all that could be rounded up for the start.

We drove out of Nanning in pouring rain in the gloomy darkness of late afternoon. Owing to heavy traffic, it took a long time to clear the dreary outer town, but as soon as we did the driver put his foot down. He may have been driving a bus, but that was incidental. He was firmly convinced it was a sports car. He zoomed up hills, roared down them and screamed around corners until, twenty kilometres out of town, we had our first casualty. We ran into and killed a buffalo that had foolishly got in our way. The bus screeched to an abrupt halt and a voracious half-hour altercation with the buffalo's owner ensued. Most of the noise was produced by our conductor. A very shrill woman, she had started nagging the driver the moment she got on the bus. I had thought, Oh, no, a back seat driver! She'll nag him all the way. And she did, in an incredibly unpleasant yappy voice that sounded like a fox terrier after a rat.

When the driver hit the buffalo, the conductor gave him a terrible tongue-lashing. Then she started on the buffalo's owner. You'd have thought it was his fault. Eventually the matter was settled. The bus crew handed over the front number plate of the bus to the buffalo's owner. I supposed this was a token of good faith and identification. Meanwhile the male passengers alighted to visit the bushes. I envied them. As the actress said to the bishop, 'That's a very handy thing to take on a picnic.'

The bus took off again. Undeterred by his recent mishap, our driver continued to go as fast as he could when the road permitted. The country we were passing through was mountainous and on the slopes that weren't wooded it was beautifully terraced. At times we climbed very high up and then descended deep down again. I saw many rice paddies and an ever-increasing number of bananas. Despite this indication that we were heading south, it was very cold, as the bus had no heating. As dark fell, we were still dropping off and picking up people along the way.

We came to a fairly big town. I still have no idea what it was, but later I realised that it was the destination on my bus ticket. I got the message when the driver and the ogress hauled me and my bags off the bus. Then they trundled me through a gauntlet of blokes who were trying to get me into their bicycle taxis. I would have made this mistake if it had not been for my helpers as I thought this must be Dhongxing. The bus crew were probably just glad to be rid of the pesky foreigner, but I was grateful for their help. I would never have found my way to Dhongxing if it were not for them. I was shepherded into the street behind the bus station where, to my surprise, I was shoved towards another bus.

I heard the word 'Dhongxing' shouted at the driver of this dilapidated old crate, and that was when it dawned on me that I was not there yet. He grabbed my bags, threw them on board, then threw me on too, grabbing and man-handling me as I went in. I had to scramble over a mountain of enormous hessian bales that blocked the aisle, but otherwise the bus was empty. The other passengers had got out for refreshments. When they returned, a woman went to sit down next to me. In the half-dark she did not realise that I was a foreigner until she got close. Then she leaped up again as if she had been shot and, with alarm on her face, shied away and was about to bolt. I smiled disarmingly, patted the seat beside me and said, 'Sit down, please.' After a bit more encouragement, she gingerly resumed her seat and gradually relaxed. Then deciding that I was innocuous, she began trying to talk to me and, smiling and laughing, was very affable.

The rest of the people on the bus, who seemed to belong to an ethnic minority group, were also very friendly. There was no conductor just a lot of self-appointed helpers and an enormous amount of baggage. The colossal lumpy bales tied up in hessian were packed all the way down the aisle, and across the back and front of the bus so that from where I sat in the second seat I could see nothing, not even the driver.

The old heap of a bus took off, the interior light went out, and we rattled slowly along through the pitch black countryside. My friendly neighbour, who was the only fat woman I saw in China, went to sleep with her head resting firmly on my shoulder and her hair mingling with mine. I hoped that nothing was ambling across this bridge from her to me. She emitted a strong smell of soap, which, when someone you don't know is sleeping on top of you, is reassuring. A few days later in Vietnam, however, I discovered that it was possibly only her clothes that gave off the strong carbolic smell and that it did not necessarily extend to her hair. My head started to itch and I realised that some of her livestock had been transferred to me. I rushed to the chemist to get something lethal to head lice. I looked up the word for them in my Vietnamese phrasebook, but the scholarly Vietnamese gentleman who had written that book had not envisaged its being used by low life who harboured walkies in their hair. In the shop I performed a charade of a flea-bitten tourist. The young girl assistant looked at me aghast, her eyes wide with horror. I hoped it was because I did not look the type for this kind of medicine. Finally we sorted out what I needed and I was washed and cleansed of my impurities.

For an hour and a half the bus banged along a bumpy track. The only town I had seen since leaving Nanning had been the one where I had changed buses. Apart from that, there had been only tiny villages and now there were not even many of those. Then we came to a military checkpoint miles from anywhere and suddenly my newfound friends, the fickle wretches, abandoned me like rats deserting a sinking ship. It was as though I had suddenly developed the plague. Shouting, 'Loala! Loala!' they stumbled over themselves to get as far away from me as possible. My erstwhile good neighbour, who only a minute before had been happily asleep on my shoulder, belted to the back of the bus. They wanted nothing to do with me in a situation where the military was involved. Foreigner might mean trouble out here.

Three heavily munitioned soldiers got on the bus and body searched all the men. Then they came to me. Two kids who looked about fifteen swung on the end of great big cannon sized sub-machine guns, while a snippy boy with pimples shouted questions at me. I understood nothing. I wanted to shout back, 'Look, sunshine. I've had a long hard day during the course of which I have been an accessory to the murder of a buffalo. It is now nine o'clock at night and my bladder is up to my eyebrows, I have no idea where I am, or for that matter where I am going or where I have been and you want to ask me stupid questions.' But all I did was smile and, as I felt that I had to answer something, I kept repeating the magic word, 'Dhongxing, Dhongxing' like a mantra.

The soldiers pointed to the pile of baggage. I presumed they were asking which was mine, so I indicated it. While they examined my bags, I wondered if this was the Vietnamese border. I hoped not. I wouldn't be allowed to pass through two days before the date on my entry visa, and there was no town nearby where I could stay.

It turned out that we were only at a Chinese military check post. There was insurrection in these parts, as well as much smuggling, and the soldiers had been looking for arms. We could have had bazookas, tanks, bodies, anything, in the massive bundles that they had failed to inspect. A little later these mysterious bales were dropped off in a village, being extracted from the bus only after much sweating effort.

By the time the bus stopped at what seemed to be the end of the road, my former fickle friends were now my chums again. Three beaming women helped me off the bus and trundled my bags across the road to what looked like a fairly upmarket establishment for way out here in the wilds. From the outside I wondered what I was stumbling into. Perhaps I had come to a brothel, or at least a nightclub. Next to the main entrance several well painted ladies hung around a very dark doorway from which loud music issued forth invitingly. The big red characters of the sign on top of the building could have said anything, disco, house of ill repute, hotel. But I figured that as my friends from the bus had steered me this way, it was probably safe.

I was halfway up the long flight of steps that led to the entrance when a small laughing man rushed down to greet me. He seemed overjoyed to see me – the only time I was welcomed in China was the last place I visited. The man grabbed my bag, shunted me up the steps and in the door and announced me, shouting what seemed to be, 'Look what I have got. A foreigner!'

All three mouths of the young women behind the counter dropped open simultaneously. They stared at me in shocked horror. They obviously didn't get many foreigners here. I said, '*Neehow*' and proved myself to be not only harmless, but friendly, and they all unfroze, became sociable and agreed to let me have a room. Until then, I had thought that I might be in a restricted area and could be refused entry to the village, or admission to a hotel. I'd had horrible visions of sitting by the side of the road on my bags for a couple of days, so I was greatly relieved.

I filled out the usual foreigner registration form and paid twenty dollars for the best room in town; they would not hear of my taking anything less. One of the receptionists – a haughty breed in most other places in China – insisted on escorting me personally to my room. Not only this, but she turned on the tap in the bathroom and stood for ages waiting for the hot water to appear. Then she demonstrated all the fittings, proving what other travellers had told me to be right – that the further south you went and the smaller the places you visited, the nicer the people were.

I surveyed the best room in town. It was fine; a big bright place with everything in reasonable condition. I went to move one of the beds, but it wouldn't budge. I thought it must be nailed to the tiled floor. Then I discovered that it was made of great planks of wood, like a stockyard fence.

All the sturdy wooden furniture was painted white and had an endearingly home-made look – the kind of thing I would have turned out at my carpentry classes years ago. Mosquito nets hung draped over the beds and the bed linen was all hand embroidered. A great deal of effort had been made to make the room look first class, but whoever had done the decor had no idea. Bright, shiny mauve frilled bedspreads with the hotel's logo embroidered on them in purple were in appalling taste and clashed violently with the other gaudy fittings. The bathroom had the usual strange plumbing and a hand shower without a holder. I pondered again why no fixture found on a wall in China was ever intact. What did they do? Swing on them? The toilet was a squat hole in the floor, but it was cleaner than most. There was no ward-robe, but the bathroom had rails on the walls with wooden clothes hangers on them which I took to indicate that this was where I was meant to hang my clothes. They would get a bit wet!

I found a pamphlet in the room that told me I was in the Dhongxing Hotel. It was only then that I was sure that I had finally made it.

The first thing I noticed about Dhongxing was the quiet. It was wonderful after some of the noisy places I had been. Looking down into the street at eleven o'clock at night I saw only the portable street stalls lit by kerosene lamps outside the bus station and a few people on foot. At two in the morning, however, I was rudely awakened by a dozen men banging on all the doors and shouting loudly. I shot up in bed thinking that the police had discovered I should not be here, had come to raid the place and were hauling everyone out looking for me. (That's what a guilty conscience does to you.) Eventually I realised that it was only a bunch of drunks returning to their rooms from the nightclub below and behaving in the usual inconsiderate manner. The deafening din continued until four in the morning. They yelled, banged on doors and shouted up and down the corridors of every floor. One of them may have been locked out of his room; at one stage I heard the sound, somewhere below, of a door being broken and demolished.

In the morning, I opened the curtains and found that they covered a big wide window through which the sun shone brightly, but which was closely barred to prevent anything else getting in. This was the first time I had seen the sun for days and it was lovely to be warm again. I had been very cold by the time I had arrived last night. There was not much pollution here, but later in the day the sky clouded over and it looked as though the rain was following me down from Nanning. I still didn't know if I was on the coast, or in the mountains, but Dhongxing was definitely a border town – I saw signs written in both Chinese and Vietnamese.

From the window I couldn't see much apart from the street and the bus station. There was little traffic; the odd bus, a few cars, some bike and other pedal power and some put-putting tractors. I liked this. The things I found hardest to contend with in China were the crowds and the traffic.

Investigating the village I found everyone charming, glad to see me and helpful. Could this still be China? Maybe I did cross over in the night! I discovered that I was only a kilometre from the Vietnamese border, but there was no such thing as a taxi in Dhongxing. I asked the girls at the hotel's reception desk to direct me to a bank. They had never heard of such a thing. I went into a place of business that looked as though it could have been a bank. It wasn't, but a young woman took me into the street, put me into a pedicab and told the rider where to take me. When I arrived at the bank, the same thing happened there. I was given explicit details of how to get somewhere to change money and I started off, but a young man from the establishment, obviously deciding that I would not find it alone, followed me out and got into the pedicab with me. He took me to a back street money changer where I got a better rate than the bank, stayed to help me with the transaction and saw that I got a good deal. When I tried to pay for the pedicab, he wouldn't take my money. I said I wanted to go on to the post office, so he took me there too, escorting me to the desk and showing me around before he left.

I wanted to mail a postcard home in time for a family member's birthday, but it appeared that I could not do it there. The assistant came from behind his counter and took me – despite the fact that the post office was a big, shiny new building, it was empty – into the building next door. But when I tried to post the card the woman presiding over this counter, who had obviously never seen a postcard before, just gazed at it in wonder. I don't think the post office did much business; I was the sole customer in here too. Fortunately, a young man came in just then who told me he had majored in English and asked if he could practise speaking it. Word was out about me. He had tracked me down from the bank. We chatted for a while and he told me that he worked for the Agricultural Bank and that the post-mistress wanted me to put my card in the envelope she was offering me. I said it was not needed. She thought I did not want to pay for the stamps on the envelope. My friend assured me, 'No problem. She says she will send it for nothing.' I said that wasn't the way it worked. I wanted to buy the stamps and put them on the postcard. I did so and passed it back to her. She franked it and then said it still had to go in an envelope. Without my friend I would never have convinced her to put it in the mail bag. It took some doing, but finally and reluctantly she did. I know she did not believe that this was the way you sent postcards, and I don't really think the young man did either. They just humoured another mad foreigner. But the postcard for my sister's birthday arrived!

Finding my way around the village was easy. It was fortunate that the hotel was opposite the bus station and that I could say 'bus station' in Chinese; it is the same as in English. I checked out the upmarket restaurant attached to the front of the hotel. It was empty, and six young lady attendants stood around doing nothing. After much talking and giggling we ordered something. It turned out to be a great amount of chicken skin, fat and splintered bones chopped into inedible clumps. It wasn't cheap either. I followed it with a fish dish which was only passable. But I ate its delicious sauce with some rice and went up the street in search of more food. On the footpath at the bottom of the steps in front of the hotel's restaurant were numerous wire cages in which the food was stored – fresh and on the hoof. There were chooks, fish and crabs in tanks, birds like fluffy pheasants and tortoises – how could they eat tortoises! Huge mounds of them with their stumpy legs waving pathetically in the air were stacked in the market.

Though at first I was put off Dhongxing by my experience of the food, I came to like it because everyone was so pleasant to me. This was a strange feeling. A congenial place with a good vibrant feeling to it, I decided Dhongxing was the best place I had been in, with the exception of Yanshu, and I spent an enjoyable couple of days there. And later I found a wonderful night market close to the hotel that was a great place to eat.

Dhongxing's streets go up hill and down dale and there are only two large ones. The rest are mostly small cobbled lanes that are sprinkled with interesting street stalls and markets. I was only one of a few foreigners seen in this village and people let me stray around unmolested. Either they were too afraid to hassle me or they were too kind. The only way to get around was by pedicab, a bicycle rickshaw, which was cheap, one yuan anywhere in town. With my weight on a flat surface, I do not find riding in this form of transport guilt inducing, but when the poor peddler started going up the hills of some of these streets, I began to worry.

The television in my room delivered the Chinese news. Although I understood little of it, I grasped one bit perfectly well. A film of a sleeper bus, charred and smoking and an ordinary bus – ditto – pranged into a couple of cars. Hospital workers were carrying heaps of bodies away. The cynics say the carnage on the road is one way of keeping the population down.

Walking past the outskirts of the village, I was immediately in the dark green of the jungle and in country very different from the China I had seen so far. At the end of a wandery, deeply rutted road I discovered a long flight of steps that went up to an ancient crumbling monument. At the top of the steps was what had once been a charming park but was now very run down. In it a couple of quaint willow pattern bridges spanned a stream near a pagoda. There was a strange feeling in this place, like being in a lost world, and I would have liked to stay for a while, but it was now dusk and I decided that it was probably no time to be rambling around in a park.

9 Heroin to Hair Oil

I was nervous about entering North Vietnam overland. Vietnam remains a police state and I was afraid that, particularly in the north, I would be viewed with animosity and suspicion. After ousting the French in 1954, the communist government isolated itself from the west. Travellers have only been gradually allowed to enter the country since 1991 and very few had come over land borders. The word 'Vietnam' was to me, as it still is to many westerners, synonymous with a dreadful and bitter war. No one ever mentioned that the country was beautiful and the people gracious, hospitable and kind. Once I realised this, the war seemed all the more terrible.

And the guidebook gave the operation of crossing a land border very bad reviews. North Vietnamese Communist officials are notoriously xenophobic and frontier guards were said to be hostile. They had been known to refuse travellers entry for no valid reason, as well as give them a hard time about the contents of their luggage. I had even risked my tape recordings in the Chinese mail rather than chance them being confiscated, as I had read could happen.

Finding transport to the border was not easy. The Dhongxing Hotel staff fielded my enquiry to a man, who directed me to a car parked at the end of the street. Its driver proved unwilling, but a spectator came to my aid and dragged me further up the road to an office that seemed to be in the bus business. Here my passport was examined at length, especially that wretched visa extension which was argued about loud and long. Finally I was told, 'No. But sit and wait.' After a while I was taken outside by a middle-aged woman, complete with her bulky knitting, who had apparently adopted my cause. With much gesticulating, my new accomplice conveyed to me that we should hire a pedicab. We did so and, returning to the hotel, collected my bags and set off. The rider pedalled us along tiny, crowded lanes that wound uphill for about a kilometre, before stopping in front of a flight of stone steps that led up to a gateway set high above the street. I'd never have guessed that this was the border. Loudly heralded by my friend, who followed behind still knitting, I climbed to the top. The Chinese Guardian of the Gate examined my passport. 'What do you want?' he asked.

'I want to go to Vietnam.'

'Enter!'

Passing through the arched stone entrance, I walked up a steep, paved incline that was overhung by big trees and flanked by garden plots bursting with flowers. My friend still tagged along. At the end of the path I came to a building that was entirely covered in dazzling, shiny blue glass, the interior of which proved to be a great echoing, almost empty hall. A charming young Chinese official greeted me and we started formalities. After questioning me at length, the official produced a form and escorted me to a desk to fill it out. Then came a bombshell. 'Can I see your vaccination certificate?' I had accidentally left that behind in Hong Kong months ago and until now had not given it another thought. No one had asked to see it when I had entered China and I wondered why they were interested in it now that I was about to leave the country. I tried to explain how I had lost it. It sounded pretty limp, but the young man said that in lieu of presenting my certificate I could make a statement about the condition of my health.

He gave me a form to fill out. It wanted to know if I was suffering from AIDS, Hepatitis B or any other undesirable disease. I thought that I'd hardly be likely to say so if I was. I vowed that I was as pure as the driven snow. This satisfied the young man and he, the trusting soul, kindly waived the requirement to produce a vaccination certificate.

Although Vietnamese and Chinese people were moving to and fro rapidly across the border outside, I received a special scrutiny and the first stage of my crossing took an hour. As few foreigners came through here, I was of great interest, as well as being a captive subject with whom the staff could practise their English. It was only after everyone in the building had played with my passport, wondered over it, handed it back and forth and I'd had a long social chat all round, that the first official said, 'Now we will move onto customs.' Expecting a gruelling inspection, I heaved my bags up onto the counter and opened them. But the customs' officer did not look at anything. He was only interested in my books. When I showed him my travel guide, his interest evaporated. No dirty pictures as he had hoped.

Finally, farewelled and sent on my way with good wishes, I stepped out into a gorgeous morning and walked easily towards Vietnam. A wide river separates Vietnam and China at this point and a long, paved bridge is the no man's land between the guard posts on each side. Crossing the bridge was an enjoyable doddle after what I had imagined awaited me – a horrible border shanty manned by thoroughly anti-social people.

Reaching the Vietnamese side, I came to a line of low adobe buildings and trundled my bags past the first guard, who did not seem the least bit interested in me. But soon someone came up behind me and said, 'In here. You wait in this room.' Long and narrow and containing only a big table surrounded by chairs, it looked like an old school room. I waited half an hour. I ate some fruit from my bag, did some knitting, read my guidebook and looked at the map on the wall. I had the feeling I was being watched to see whether I got nervous and betrayed any sinister motives.

Eventually a good-looking young gent wearing an army uniform and with a great-coat thrown over his shoulders in the manner of Hitler's SS sauntered in, sat down and had a chat with me. I wasn't sure if he was the immigration official or a visitor. He looked like a captain, so I addressed him as such and he did not argue. Finally he reached for my passport and copied my details into a very old, battered exercise book. No computers here. As I filled out the innumerable forms that he kept pushing towards me across the table, the captain continued to question me.

Then he asked me if I had anything to declare. I asked what sort of things he had in mind. 'Like jewellery,' he said and I replied, 'No.'

'Camera?'

'Yes.'

'Video?'

'No.' Then he said, 'Do you have anything prohibited, like hair oil?' I looked at him dumbfounded. I couldn't believe my ears. I asked him to repeat it and he said, more clearly, 'Her oin.'

'No.' I said, and burst out laughing.

'Cocaine?' he said, and I laughed again. I think that my giggles may have convinced him that I was merely an innocent tourist, but it really was ridiculous. Immigration officials don't usually ask if you have heroin in your luggage, or even hair oil. But there was a funny, cold hard look in his eyes and I thought, God help me if I did.

After this the Captain said that I was finished and asked me if there was anything I would like to ask *him* or if I wanted anything written down to help me on my way. How kind, I thought, and said that I would appreciate directions to where I could get a bus to Haiphong. I knew a train ran from there to Hanoi. The captain recommended that I stop at Halong Bay on my way south, saying that it was a very beautiful place and I should not miss it. It was here that I discovered that I was almost on the coast.

I said, 'Do I go to customs now?' But he replied, 'No, you may go.' Apparently he was the lot rolled into one. So much for the traumatic searches I had dreaded, I was through! It had taken over two hours but had been no trouble at all.

Outside, I was on Vietnamese soil. Good-bye to China!

Hoping to find some transport to the village of Mong Cai, a kilometre or so further on, where the Captain had said that I would find a bus, I started walking down the dirt road. The only vehicles I came upon were several old army trucks that now seemed to be in the general carrier business and gave off a powerful pong of pig. I showed the paper with my directions written on it to a man sitting beside one of the trucks. He signaled to someone. Up roared a motorbike and, before I knew it, the rider had grabbed me and hustled me onto the pillion. Heaving my big bag up in front of him on the petrol tank, he shoved the smaller bag between us and thundered off, with me clutching my handbag, the bag in front of me and the rider, and shrieking, 'Slowly! Slowly!'

Later I laughed to think that I had left China by bicycle and entered Vietnam on a motorbike.

We travelled a couple of kilometres in this precarious manner and then I was deposited by the roadside. A minivan screeched to a halt at my feet. The tiny vehicle was already squashed full, but I was forcibly crammed into the back seat. They not only bundled me in, but added several more people afterwards. Then a few metres further on a man hailed the bus and wanted the driver to take a bicycle aboard – a spanking new bike with big wire carrier baskets front and back. I thought, You've got to be joking. But they weren't. They got it in! The driver produced a wrench, took off the bike's front wheel and put the dismantled parts between the first two seats. The passengers in the second seat rode for more than six hours with a bike on their laps. It seemed to me that the bus was now way past full, but a short distance beyond this point we picked up one more woman. She was squeezed in beside me so that we only had half a buttock each on the seat. Now the van which had been designed to carry eight passengers bulged with fifteen people, baggage, freight and a bike. The last woman to get on, who was about thirty years old, took one look at me as the bus moved off and burst into tears. I thought, Oh, come on, I'm not that bad. But she sobbed on and on, utterly breaking her heart and only stopping occasionally to wipe her nose on her sleeve. I figured that she didn't have a hanky, so I groped in my bag, got out my wad of precious toilet paper, passed it to her and she continued to snivel in that.

We hadn't gone far when the bus blew a tyre and all the passengers had to get out and sit on the side of the road while the wheel was changed. Then we were herded back in and continued on until we came to a boom gate that had been lowered to halt us at a check point. This place looked like something out of a cowboy film – a fort at the Mexican border. The only thing missing was a bloke sitting against the outside wall with a sombrero over his face. A rough wooden fence encircled a low, white-washed building that was surrounded by a rickety, thatched verandah held up by crooked posts that had been made from narrow tree trunks. Woven rattan had been tacked between the posts to enclose the sides of the verandah and a Vietnamese flag flapped lazily from a sapling anchored in the baked, flattened earth of the courtyard.

The passengers were ejected from the bus to be checked over; the men and the vehicle were thoroughly body searched. The soldiers even inspected under the bus's engine. Luckily we passed the test and were allowed to drive on. Leaving the yard we came to the boom gate. Our driver got out, lifted it up himself and we were off again. By this time my weeping neighbour had exhausted her passions. Now she turned her attention to a mammoth stick of sugar cane that she had brought along as solace. She chopped and chomped this in my ear until, having totally worn herself out, she went to sleep on my shoulder, only waking now and then for a further sniffle. I could feel the dampness of her tears seeping through my shirt, but by the time she got off the bus she had recovered and my shirt was dry.

On and on, along shocking dirt roads, the bus bumped and jolted in clouds of dust with all the windows down. I had no idea how far it was to where I was going. In fact, I had no idea where I was going at all! I hoped we would stop soon though, because my bladder had started to demand attention.

It actually took six hours to reach Halong Bay. At first the countryside wasn't all that different from China – rice grew lushly in paddies and there were fields of waving green sugar cane. But the housing was very different. It had become far more picturesque. Among the fields I saw adobe houses and quaint little places of atap, woven palm and rattan. The villages were a haphazard arrangement of either diminutive square houses or the same tiny houses that were another two or three storeys higher.

After a while we came to low terraced hills and further on heavily wooded mountains that were too steep for crops or gardens. Three-quarters of Vietnam consists of mountains and hills. The Truong Son Mountains, which form the central highlands, run from the north, where they are covered with snow for most of the year, almost the length of the entire country, as well as sending out spurs that continue eastwards to the coast. Vietnam is also a land of much water. Apart from the two great river systems, the Red River in the north and the Mekong in the south, many rivers originate in the mountains and flow across the country and into the

South China Sea. We crossed several of these rivers that had picturesque villages clinging to their sides.

I noticed that the people on this side of the border generally seemed more handsome than the Chinese. Many of the women were beautiful. Both men and women wore dark trousers and loose fitting tops and most people wore wide, conical-shaped, woven straw hats. One of the first things I had noticed when I had come over the border from China was the different head gear worn by the Vietnamese. Apart from straw hats, many men sported small green pith helmets that were left-overs from the days of the Viet Cong.

Later the road followed the coast for some time and as sunset approached I realised that I must be at Halong Bay. There was a photo of it in my guidebook and it was unmistakable. Thousands of tiny, pointed islands thrust straight up out of the sea, the way that the mountains of Guilin stick up out of the land. They are the same karst construction, and resemble a Chinese ink painting, but the sea surrounding them gave them an added beauty. Ha Long means 'dragon descending' and the legend that explains this unique aquatic terrain is that a great dragon spat out pearls as it plunged into the sea from its home in the mountains.

In the main street of Halong Bay's principal village, called Bai Chay, I fell out of the bus to be welcomed by a reception party of motorbikes. By this time I was about to collapse from exhaustion, not to mention the state of my bladder, so I let one rider take me where he chose. The small hotel he picked was conveniently situated one street back from the water's edge. It was ominously called Dung Phong, but it looked like a tall narrow wedding cake. The hotel foyer that doubled as the owners' living room was only four metres wide, but it encompassed the entire façade of the establishment. From the centre of the foyer a narrow, spiral stone staircase wound up through the minute hotel to the eight guest rooms, two of which occupied each floor.

I was gasping for the drink the hotel's owners gave me as we bargained amicably until a suitable price was reached. It had come as a shock to be cordially welcomed by people who seemed happy to see me. I creaked upstairs – many stairs, shades of China – to my room which was on the fourth floor. Desperate to get to the bathroom, I had to practically throw the man who had accompanied me out, but eventually he got the message.

I received another shock, a disagreeable one this time, when I looked in the mirror. An escapee from the black and white minstrel show stared back at me. Except for white circles where my sun-glasses had been, I was covered in dirt, and from the white circles my eyes peered out of an almost black visage. My hair, now pale brown, stood on end thick with dust. When I wiped my face the towel came away black. My once-pink shirt was now brown with black streaks. I marvelled at the politeness of the people downstairs, who had contrived not to burst out laughing at the sight of me.

My small hotel room, with its narrow casement windows and patterned glass and draw-string curtains, had a rather French air. Everything in the room worked and was squeaky clean. The toilet flushed successfully, none of the plumbing needed repairing and, wonder of wonders, the fitting on the wall that held the shower was intact. *And* I was trusted with a whole roll of toilet paper all to myself. There was even a small, coloured television set, a test drive of which produced a hilarious old silent French film. But the electric hot water service required a degree in engineering to work and through the open, unscreened window mozzies as big as Pegasus roared in. To combat them a mosquito net had been provided, but it took me a while to detect it. The net had been artfully secreted in an oblong perspex box on the wall above the bed-head and initially I had thought this was a light and spent some time trying unsuccessfully to turn it on.

Looking down from the windows of my eyrie, I saw, directly beneath me, a vivid, miniature street that was full of life. But I got vertigo looking groundwards. The windowsill was below my knees and under my feet there was an unscreened drop of four floors which seemed very dangerous. Only a few feet away, opposite my window, I was confronted by one of the towering, pointy mountains that had escaped the sea to erupt on the land. A row of whimsical, high but narrow houses had been built against the mountain's sides and my room was level with the balconies of their upper storeys. Downstairs, I intimated that I needed feeding. The hotel owner took me next door to a diminutive café and handed me over to a friend. The café's name was Dung Dung Fuk and its proprietor told me proudly that he had named his little girl after it. Poor kid. The Vietnamese language has some unfortunate English connotations. I discovered that I was now in a country whose currency was called dong and whose national dish is po. The café owner's elderly father greeted me enthusiastically in French. Many older Vietnamese still speak French and they think that any educated foreigner does too. Stumbling along with the few thoroughly flawed words of school-girl French that I still retain and drawing pictures, I managed to communicate with him.

The café's fittings were basic: rough wooden benches and long communal wooden tables. The cooking was done on a coal burner on the street front. I dined well on crunchy, deep fried prawns, small cold fish in a delicious spicy sauce and vegetables. I sampled the local beer. It was good and cheap.

Then mine host produced someone who spoke English to entertain me: (or find out about me) a young man who was the manager of the government-owned hotel across the street. He was the only one on duty, so he kept his eye on his hotel foyer from where we sat. Toi said that his hotel had ten rooms which cost ten dollars each, but that their main business was import and export. Strange business for a hotel.

From the time that I had arrived in Bai Chay I had been forced to listen to the propaganda broadcast that boomed from a loud speaker in the nearby public square. I asked Toi what it was. 'It's government news,' he said. Whether you want it or not, I thought. The Vietnamese were apparently as much into this form of entertainment/torture as the Chinese.

A little later I fell into bed and was fast asleep at once. But I was woken shortly afterwards. I had thought I'd found a nice quiet place, but Vietnamese on holiday proved to be just as noisy as the Chinese. They shouted, yahooed and slammed doors in the middle of the night and the distur-bance reverberated up the stone staircase as though it was an echo chamber. Then someone threw on the landing light as well as the light in the room opposite mine and left them on all night. My room had a glass door. I got up to hang a blanket over it. At half past five in the morning the propaganda merchant started screaming and yelling over the loud speaker again and after that I got no more sleep. I was not amused.

In the café Dung Dung Fuk I enjoyed a traditional Vietnamese breakfast, while trying not to watch the dishes being washed in the gutter at the front of the establish-ment. Most small places had no water and the only running water available to them was in the gutters. Breakfast con-sisted of a big bowl of thick noodles mixed with whatever had been left over from last night's dinner and topped with a tasty sauce, a squeeze of juice from a tiny green lime and a dash of chopped chilli. It was one of the best breakfasts I'd had while travelling and it only cost a few cents. I was still feeling sleepy, but some great, strong heart-starting Vietnamese coffee soon fixed that. Then the itinerant butcher called at the café. He carried his wares in an old, cane basket which he put on the ground and everyone came and handled the meat. I went for a walk.

Having heard that jewellery shops were the places to change money quietly, I patronised one in the main street where a genial woman gave me a good rate of exchange. Next I went in search of the wharf from where the boat sailed down the coast to Haiphong. Vietnam is a long and narrow country that lies between the Tropic of Cancer and the Equator, and, although it is only fifty kilometres wide in places, it stretches for over 1700 kilometres along the Indochinese Peninsula and has borders with Cambodia, Laos and China as well as 3260 kilometres of coastline.

At the crossroads of Bai Chay's two main streets, I noticed a big round communal well surrounded by cement where women washed themselves, their clothes, their dishes and their babies. Wandering on I went into many places that I probably should not have, was offered a ride on a sampan around the harbour and found the ferry that went over to the island across the bay, but I didn't find the wharf.

Although almost no one spoke English, everyone I met was sociable. The hotel owner's mother tried very hard to talk to me. She really wanted to get to know me. On my second morning, deeply concerned about my health, she took my hand, looked intently into my face, and asked me if I had slept better. When I said that I had, she seemed genuinely pleased. I now wished I'd spent my entire time travelling in Vietnam.

But Vietnam also had its drawbacks. Rubbish abounded in the streets of Bai Chay and mean-looking dogs scavenged through piles of it in the gutters. And once more I was appalled at the mindless cruelty I saw inflicted on animals. One day I watched two poor live birds, with an awful hopeless look in their eyes, being dragged along the street as a toy on a string by a child.

I had slept better the second night, but there was no way

of getting away from the morning's harangue. It battered its way through ear plugs and shut windows and seeped into your subconscious. Sounding like a loud barrage of exhortations and demands, it continued non-stop, hammering the senses in a violent assault. The locals seemed oblivious to it. Maybe you got used to it like you did the call to prayer in Muslim countries. Downstairs, in the room open to the street at the front of the hotel where the owners sat in the evening, it almost drowned out the television. The harangue worked in one way though; it had me up by seven o'clock every morning. Even at this early hour the street below me was alive with activity.

At last I located the wharf. It was a rusting metal pier that was punctuated by holes big enough to give vistas of the water below. The boats tied to it were not much better. They looked precariously dilapidated and a particularly decrepit wreck of wood and iron turned out to be the one on which I was to sail. Myriads of small boats plied the water between the mainland and the islands around the bay, and there was a constant coming and going of sampans and bigger wooden boats shaped like Chinese junks, complete with children, dogs and pot plants – one even sported a small tree.

After three days in Bai Chay, I said my farewells at the hotel and climbed onto a motorbike. I had discovered that this was the only means of transport here, apart from the use of your feet. 1000 dong, or ten cents, got you a big thank you, as well as the price of a ride anywhere around town. I was getting good at managing motorbike transport, which I once heard referred to as 'transpiration'. Did that mean inspirational transport? The riders here went very slowly and sedately when I was on the pillion. I hoped this was because they had learned that tourists who were unused to Asian road rules had more delicate nervous systems and not in deference to my great age.

In the old stone building that served as the waiting room and ticket office on the wharf, I paid the fare to Haiphong – much to the amusement of the female officer who wrote my name and nationality in the tattered school exercise book that housed the official foreigners' dossier. I wondered why she found it so funny that I was travelling by ship and why tabs were kept on foreigners. Was it in case one went missing, possibly drowned? The ticket to Haiphong cost 50,000 dong, which sounds like a fortune, but was only five dollars. I rattled down the pier, passed the two ticket collectors who tried on my hat with much hilarity, and clattered onto the boat.

Our ancient craft set sail and lumbered along hugging the coast. In the three and a half hours it took to reach Haiphong we never left sight of the shore, which, in view of the vessel's age and condition, seemed a very wise precaution. I sat on a hard, shiny wooden bench. The sides of the boat were lined by windows which contained no such refinement as glass. A pretty Vietnamese student seated herself opposite me and began to practise her English. She told me she was too young to marry yet, but that she would do so when she was twenty-five and then she would have three children. I asked her if the number of children allowed was government controlled and she said no, but that the ideal was two. I read that despite long years of war, famine and mass emigration, Vietnam is one of the most populous countries in the world and that, in a land a little smaller than Italy, there are over sixty-four million people, half of whom are under twenty years of age. When I discovered that the student sitting with me was also studying Chinese, I gave her my Chinese phrase book. I had no intention of using it again.

Despite the decrepitude of our antiquated boat, it still ran to first and second classes, which were divided by a narrow walkway through its centre. In this passage-way a young woman set up a low wooden table and several microscopic stools, produced a kerosene-powered stove, laid out an array of jars, bowls and bottles containing various edibles and cooked and fed passengers who came and sat down with her two or three at a time. It looked a very sociable and agreeable manner of dining. All over Vietnam I was to see women arrive with two baskets on a shoulder pole and set up these instant portable restaurants on the street.

The boat trip beat travelling by over-crowded bus on the terrible roads and the scenery was wonderful. For the first hour we passed slowly among the thousands of mountain islets, each surrounded by a flotilla of boats, which rise like the Loch Ness monster out of the sea over an area of 1500 square kilometres. Their fantastic shapes and the wondrous grottos they contain have given them their unusual names such as 'the unicorn' and 'fighting cocks'.

Haiphong had been given bad press in my travel guide, but I found it extremely acceptable. The moral of this is that you shouldn't believe everything you read in travel books. Haiphong is charming. About 100 kilometres east of Hanoi, it was just a sleepy market town until the French arrived. Now it is the major port of the north. Haiphong has witnessed the coming and going of many conquerors, the last being the Japanese, and it was heavily bombed by the Americans in their war with Vietnam. Full of interesting, old French colonial-era buildings, it has no traffic to speak of except that which is propelled by pedal power.

I took a cyclo, the first pedicab I had seen in this country, from the boat to the train station. The streets of Haiphong are wide, it was a heavenly, sunny day with a gentle breeze and it was altogether delightful to be pushed about in something that resembled a hybrid of a wheel barrow, a bath chair and an oversized pram. That is, after I had overcame the initial feeling that I looked a complete fool in it. Vietnamese cyclos have seats that tilt back, so that you either have to perch uncomfortably on their edges, or loll back like the Sheik of Araby. I am a loller by nature, so I had no difficulty with this part. The problem was that the cyclo had no sides or top, only wooden arm rests, and I was projected out in front of the vehicle like a roo bar to cushion the driver if we hit anything. I felt like the ultimate air bag. This was not too bad here, where the traffic was light, but later in Saigon it became nerve-racking. I would see doom approaching me in the form of a thousand whizzing motor-bikes as the rider pushed me, his buffer, feet first across a wide, busy intersection against the flow of the oncoming traffic. Bikes would graze past and ricochet off me as the traffic and I came together in the middle of the road in a panic-inducing *danse macabre*. I noted that cyclo riders were invariably young (maybe they don't live long enough to get old) and cheerful. They should be, *they* didn't have a lot to worry about!

The Haiphong train station was an airy colonial building and there were no crowds or barricades. The cyclo rider carried my bags into the station and waited to see that I was able to buy a ticket before he left. At the counter an obliging woman served me and I met a young New Zealander – the first westerner I had come across since Yanshu. The train to Hanoi, with its cheerful blue and yellow carriages, stood alongside the station platform, but it was several hours before departure time, so I looked after Tony's bags while he walked to the market to buy provisions.

He returned with a delicious stick of French bread and cheese, salami, pork paste and fruit, all of which had cost two dollars. We bought drinks at the kiosk bar in the main hall where the locals waited and moved into the 'Tourist Waiting Room' – a place set aside from the proletariat – to have a picnic. The Vietnamese government also discriminates against foreigners. They had tourist prices, a device probably copied from the Chinese, but at least they offered you something extra for it. The Tourist Waiting Room, which was situated on one side of the station building, was not very big, but this was something I now appreciated. It was also extremely comfortable, with good-quality leather armchairs set around a large coffee table that was graced by a tea set and thermos. A luggage storage unit covered all of one wall. An antique wooden cabinet with bevelled edges and an elegant patina, it would have looked great in any house. A female guard kept us company in the waiting room. She was soon joined by many of her friends, workers in railway uniforms, and they had beer all round – several times. I hoped none of them was driving the train.

But the train station had no toilet. You had to walk across the road to a public convenience in the square which was *al fresco* in every way. Not only was it roofless and open to the elements, but it had no partitions for privacy. There were not even any holes in the ground. You squatted on a sloping tiled floor behind which a ditch ran away downhill.

The ticket seller had sworn that there was nothing available on this train except hard-class seats, so Tony and I boarded the train with hard-class tickets. But the carriage our seats were in actually turned out to be soft class. Bliss. Everyone had a seat and no luggage clogged the aisle. All surplus baggage was in the conductor's den. He seemed to be running an unofficial freight business on the side. He also seemed to be giving his friends free or subsidised rides; three of them were squeezed in with the freight.

A gaggle of French tourists, who had obviously mis-spent several hours waiting for the train in the pursuit of the grape in some hostelry, were seated near us. They had not been terribly attractive to begin with, but as the booze got to their bladders and they rocked and rolled down the carriage in search of the toilet, they became ludicrous. One man looked like a dim-witted dancing bear and a woman wore shorts. She did not have the figure to wear them anywhere, but she should have been forcibly restrained from wearing them in Vietnam where this fashion is seen as flagrantly immoral. It often appeared to me that many tourists on short package trips did not bother to find out anything about the culture of the countries they were to visit – unlike most individual travellers who need to do so for self-preservation.

Darkness soon fell and I couldn't see much from the train windows. A metal trolley trundled through the carriage aisle dispensing tea from big tin kettles and two hours after leaving Haiphong we crossed a massive bridge over the Red River. Then we were running into Hanoi.

10 Hanoi

Life began in Vietnam in the Ma River valley, south-west of Hanoi, about 500,000 years ago. By the third millennium BC, the Lac Viets, who were the direct ancestors of modern Vietnamese, had developed a highly complex and sophisticated society. In 111 BC the Red River area in the north was invaded and subjugated by Han Chinese, who named it Nam Viet, The South Land. It took a thousand years, but finally in 939 AD, a Vietnamese general ousted the Chinese and laid the foundation for the independent state of Vietnam.

Another thousand years followed, this time of independence, until the French came – first missionaries in the seventeenth century, and then, in the nineteenth century, merchants who wanted to set up trading posts. The Vietnamese resisted with guerilla warfare, but by 1893 the French had secured the entire Indochinese Peninsula.

When the Japanese invaded Indochina in the second world war, the Viet Minh guerilla fighters, who were led by Ho Chi Minh, turned their anti-colonial nationalism against these new imperialist enemies. The French collaborated with the Japanese and were allowed to continue ruling Vietnam, so the Viet Minh fought both the French and the Japanese with aid supplied by China and the United States.

After the war, Ho Chi Minh set up the Democratic Republic of Vietnam in Hanoi and became its first president. When the British permitted French rule again in the south, war erupted between the north and the south.

In 1949 the US responded to a French request for help in the war, but in 1954 the Viet Minh defeated the French. Vietnam was then divided into the communist north and a puppet government, that was controlled by the US and which persecuted communist sympathisers, in the south. US strength in Vietnam gradually increased and by 1962 bombing and artillery began which sometimes wiped out entire villages. Millions died. In 1975 the Viet Minh won the American war and the country was united. The US placed an embargo on the country, which was not lifted until 1994. Twenty years later the Vietnamese bear no grudges.

A line of cyclos waited in front of the Hanoi railway station. Being gently pedalled through the spacious, tree-lined streets in the tepid softness of the night air was lovely. There was no wind, just the breeze made by our movement among the sparse traffic. I followed Tony to the Trung Guest House where he had previously stayed and which he highly recommended. The ingenious child-like girl who was in charge of this establishment greeted Tony warmly. At first she said, 'Dormitory okay for Tony. No room for you.' Then, as it was late and I said I was tired, she phoned the boss and came back with, 'Okay, room for you.'

The Trung guest house was another of those tiny places. Thin but tall, its three storeys had been altered and added to wherever possible. Hanoi obviously had no town planning officials to inhibit such expression. The Trung was weird, but agreeable and extremely cheap. My six-dollar room was merely a cranny that had been created in the corridor, but it was clean, comfortable and had a good bed. In a former existence it had been the space under the stairs and the 'roof' sloped down over the bed that had just managed to compress itself into the length of the room. A tiny table alongside the bed and a hole in the wall that had been fitted with two shelves was the sum total of the furnishings. The room was partitioned from the passage by colour-bond silver garage metal to waist level and opaque glass from there. A sliding door completed the picture. There was no window. A small exhaust fan in the partition over the foot of the bed pulled air in from the dormitory next door and saved the occupant from asphyxiation. There were gaps where the metal did not meet the wall and the construction was very rough and ready.

This little house was so safe that you did not need to lock anything except against your fellow-travellers. The room keys hung where everyone could get at them and you just helped yourself. An honour box stood by the phone and, remarkably, you kept your own tab in an exercise book that had your room number on it. It was up to you to enter how much you owed for food, drinks and laundry. One visitor went to Halong Bay for three days and was told to pay when he got back. Such trust was astounding, especially after China's paranoid conviction that all travellers only came there to steal the bed linen.

The Trung's dormitory contained a row of two-tiered bunks that made it look like a railway sleeping carriage. The communal sitting-dining room at the front of the guest house was furnished with good-quality, carved Gothic chairs, settee and table. One corner was occupied by an altar that was always well supplied with burning joss sticks, fruit and flowers. A tiny kitchen with just enough space for one person to stand in was attached to one side of the room. Food was served through a hatch in the wall, but the only way to enter the kitchen was through a doorway in the street which you had to go out the front door to reach. The staff at the Trung were genuine people who didn't do things for you just because you were paying them. They reminded me of the Balinese. The hotel owner was a gentle and charming doctor of medicine. Her business cards not only advertised the hotel's allures, but offered 'free health care' to guests. She said her husband, who was also a doctor, could supply me with some more anti-malarials. I met him later. A gracious man in army uniform, he told me that he was not practising medicine now. He was studying computer programming. I was glad to hear it. The tablets he gave me were Chloroquine and everyone knows that Vietnam's mosquitoes are resistant to it. I found it intriguing that although he wore an army uniform and must have been officially a communist his wife burned joss on her altar.

The Trung staff consisted of Ngon, a beautiful and serene woman who did the cooking and cleaning and who said she was thirty-nine, but looked more like seventeen and Tham, the joyful and very competent roustabout who lived on the premises and slept on the settee in the front room so that she could let the guests in at night. She vowed she was eighteen, but she looked about twelve. I would like to have bottled whatever ran in the genes of these two females.

The first morning I appeared alongside Ngon as she bent over the wash tub. Looking up, she saw me and said, 'Oh! Beautiful.' It was fresh paint, that's all, and I said so, which made her laugh and laugh.

I toddled out to inspect Hanoi by cyclo. Slowing winding through the streets on a glorious sunny late autumn day was pure bliss. The colonial building that housed the post office looked nothing like the stereotype of these places. Its semi-circular façade was approached by an impressive flight of steps. Inside a massive wooden counter stretched the width of the room and comfortable lounge chairs surrounded a low circular table in its centre. But there were no customers, the place was empty. Although the post office had an official money-changing facility, it was also where the illegal black market money merchants, who loitered outside on the steps, accosted likely clients. They would even follow you inside and sit down companionably beside you in the easy chairs to make their offers. I was joined by two of these sharp operators who, despite the presence of the staff and the uniformed guard, openly flashed wads of dong at me as they solicited my custom.

Opposite the post office, peace can be found in the busiest centre of town in the tranquil park that surrounds a wonderful big lake. Called the Restored Sword Lake, it has a legend similar to that of King Arthur and his Excalibur. Crowning a tiny island in the middle of the lake and reflected in its waters is the elegant three-tiered Turtle Pagoda that seems to rise from the mists of the lake. It can be reached across the curved Rainbow Bridge, whose entrance is guarded by two towers, The Pen and Ink-slab Towers. One is pointed in the shape of a brush, the other is a hollowed rock in the form of a peach that is supported by three frogs. On the fifth day of the fifth month, the morning sun makes the shadow of the brush point dip deep into the centre of the peach ink-slab.

Revelling in the glow of the dazzling day, I wandered around the lake looking at the wares of hawkers under the brilliant flame trees and willows. I bought bananas from a woman swinging along with two baskets of fruit on her shoulder pole and was forced by necessity to patronise a public loo. It was not free. I was charged Tourist Price, 2000 dong, to use a grotty hole in the ground.

I was resting on one of the many lake-side seats when an enterprising street kid who was selling postcards approached me. I told him that what I really wanted was Lonely Planet's Guide to Vietnam which wasn't available in the shops. He said I should meet him there the next day. I did and he had acquired a second-hand one for me.

Hanoi, 'The City in the Bend of the River', has been inhabited since neolithic times, but by 1010 AD it had been established as the capital of the country. Originally just a collection of villages clustered around a walled palace on the Red River, from 1902 it was the capital of French Indochina. Most of North Vietnam is mountainous, so the Red River delta, which is the fertile rice basket of the country, is of vital importance. The river originates in the Chinese province of Hunnan, forms part of the Vietnamese Chinese border and then empties into the Gulf of Tonkin.

I found Hanoi, with its air of a provincial French town of the 1930s, incredibly interesting. I loved the colourful red and purple bougainvilleas and the lovely old buildings. Some restored, some crumbling, they were a mixture of mellow-toned oriental, eighteenth and nineteenth century European styles and the now familiar narrow, three and four storeyed houses.

On my second day at the Trung I moved up to an exclusive eight-dollar room. You had to be slim and agile to reach this garret. The tiled staircase leading to it went up almost vertically from one side of the communal front room. Inside, a sloping ceiling came down to meet white-washed walls, one of which contained a metal framed piece of opaque glass. This opened into the dormitory below and was the room's only window, as well as the air supply. I had to climb onto the bed to get at my clothes. They hung on a hook board which was nailed to the wall that the bed was against. I wondered why it had been put in such an inconvenient spot when plenty of other wall space was available.

This was the only room I have ever been in where I could not see the door when I was in bed. It was below floor level. On the far side of the room an unprotected flight of steps led to the wooden louvered door that opened onto the outside staircase. The door and entrance were so narrow that a fatty would not have got in. Shiny green and red ceramic tiles covered the floor and the stairs. It wouldn't have done to sleep walk or stumble about in the dark.

Outside, another flight of stairs went up to the bathroom at such an acute angle that I had to jump to get across to them. None of the stairs had rails.

The bath and toilet were pristine. But the toilet roll holder was fixed to the wall at head height when standing up and the shower was positioned over the bath at a level that required you to sit crosslegged sideways in the bath to get under it.

I visited the History Museum, one of Hanoi's stunning old buildings. Colonial elegance on a grand scale, it was surrounded by huge trees and green gardens of palms and frangipanis. A three-tiered entry hall soared to a peak from which a stupendous chandelier was suspended. From the tiled floor graceful columns rose that were the same soft golden tone as the walls. Wooden-framed French doors were strategically positioned between the exhibits to give views of the garden. The original hand-made glass in the doors gave the garden a wavy, unfocused look that added authenticity to the building's antiquated aura.

I strolled along the museum's spacious open halls. This day the weather had changed and it was very cold inside the high-ceilinged building. I had hoped to see some of the fine antique porcelain that Vietnam is famous for, but I was disappointed. There were a few pieces labelled 'From a sunk boat in the bottom of the sea'; but it was poor quality stuff that had been degraded by its long immersion. Among the historic exhibits I was treated to were 'Implements of French Aggression and Oppression', which included the guillotine, handcuffs and photos of an execution by firing squad. Further on I came to a door bearing the sign, 'Vistors are prayed not to enter'.

In the streets of Hanoi I saw much evidence of free enterprise. Vendors sat on footpaths with goods on bamboo trays or they pedalled and peddled. It was amazing what you could buy off a bike: clothes, plastic buckets, clothes pegs, hats, umbrellas. At the guest house, Ngon the cook did not need to go out to shop; the kitchen supplies – bread, fresh baked long sticks or rolls and meat and vegetables were all brought to the door in two baskets that hung either end of the sellers' shoulder poles.

Noisy propaganda dogged me still. In Hanoi there was no escaping it. It not only blared out from the street morning and evening, but was mobile as well. Every now and then I came across a man wheeling slowly through the streets and markets on a bicycle while he played a tape recording of the harangue through a megaphone.

Hanoi streets had few cars, but there were many bicycles and motorbikes. Cyclos were the way to get about. Almost everyone and everything was transported by some form of pedal power. Once I saw a full-sized dressing table, complete with two attached cheval mirrors, mounted on a bike and another time I saw a woman with a wire-netting chicken coop on board. She was selling miserable-looking live chooks – meat on the hoof, or bike – door to door. Another woman had a cargo of live ducks, with their feet tied together, in a wicker basket on the back of her bike, while a large murderous-looking knife lay across the handlebars.

The pharmacy displayed all its medicines in glass cases and antibiotics and other drugs, which should have been refrigerated, lay in direct sunshine at the front of the shop. Prices, which were mostly very cheap, had been clumsily handwritten with ink on old pieces of paper. You could buy anything your heart desired (except anti-malarials) – intra-muscular or intravenous Cortisone, Haloperidol, hormones. They had never heard of prescriptions. Want to give yourself an anaesthetic? No problem. You could buy the Pentothal and then the equipment with which to administer it.

Busy shops and bustling markets abounded. Most shops were small, some were mere cubicles and all the shops that sold the same item were collected together in one street as though they believed that there was safety in numbers. French perfume was a reasonable price and in some shops I saw a few things that were proudly labelled 'Made in America'. Apparently there were no hard feelings, especially in the matter of trade.

Little dogs that resembled Maltese terriers and were meant to be white scrounged among mountainous piles of garbage in the gutters, although I did see the streets being cleaned by council workers. But life went on in the gutters of Hanoi; in one a woman did her washing in a big aluminium bowl and the barber cut hair and threw shaving water down into another. Bamboo bongs, or puffs on extremely unhygienic looking communal ones the size of drain pipes, were sold at street corners.

I often ate at the Old Darling Café, a traveller's hang-out in a small down-town side street. While waiting for my meal I usually let a shoe-shine boy clean and polish my daggy old shoes, even though they were suede. I felt sorry for the many young boys who approached travellers with postcards or shoe-shine boxes. But there were few beggars on the streets of Hanoi and the ones I did see were mostly old or disabled. One day as I ate my lunch of fried rice and spicy chicken, I was entertained by the sight of a young woman nit-picking another's hair in front of her shop across the street. Business must have been slow. It could get slower if the customers saw this.

Vietnamese food is very good and incredibly cheap. The bread was divine, a legacy of the French, as was the coffee. And there was cheese, real cheese, also a left-over from French days. At the Trung, the cook used to heat the breakfast bread rolls on the coals of the cooking brazier, which made them even better.

One day, hopeful of finding a ship in which to travel down the coast to Ho Chi Minh City or other places south, I took a cyclo and went looking for the docks. I ended up lost on a dirt road. A man and woman on a motorbike stopped to ask if they could help me. This happened several times and kind passers-by directed me ever further on, until I found a boat that made short trips on the Red River. All further enquiries concerning shipping resulted in dead ends, so the next morning I went to the train station to buy a ticket south. I had decided to go to Danang by train and then on to Hoian, an ancient town I wanted to see, by bus. The station is located on Grass Street, a main road that used to run to the imperial palace and was broad enough to accommodate a parade of horses and elephants carrying high officials to an audience with the king. The street got its name from the feed for the animals that was cut by prisoners and stacked by the roadside.

At the station I found the abominable Foreigner Prices listed again. The fare to Danang was more than half a million dong. A patient woman sold me a ticket, and addressed me as 'Madame', another legacy of the French. There was even a computer. The waiting room was labelled, 'The Room for Passengers at the Train on the Station'. It had big polished wooden seats, a bar where refreshments were sold and was gratifyingly spacious and almost empty.

I went to the Hanoi Zoo. A great spot in the outer suburbs, bad luck it was not as nice for the animals as it was for the humans. The first animal I saw on entering the grounds was a big black bear chewing a plastic drink bottle that someone had thoughtfully thrown at it. Three elephants, graded in sizes, very large, medium and baby, were chained separately in an enclosure and swung their trunks ceaselessly in an agony of boredom. But one lucky one was free, although alone, in a large enclosure with a pool. I watched four men scale the wall to enter the pen with the chained ones and thought it was unfortunate that the elephants could not get at them. Other animals were taunted and provoked. Monkeys were hit, poked, prodded and teased. A tiny, trusting baby monkey with a wizened face and innocent eyes was given a lighted cigarette by a ten-year-old boy who shouldn't have been smoking anyway – although it was common to see male children doing this. I gave the horrible kid a verbal beating and would have followed it with a clip under the ear if I hadn't been afraid of getting arrested for imperialist aggression. More fortunate monkeys were being fed sugared popcorn.

This made me feel hungry. I smelled something cooking and followed my nose past the many small stalls that sold drinks and sweets until I spotted a line of cabbages on top of a crumbly wall. I thought that a source of nourishment might lie behind this barrier. I was right. Under a trellis of blue creepers nestled a tiny outdoor café. I sat down at a microscopic table on an even smaller chair and was fed big chunks of tomatoes and potatoes in a delicious soup, fried rice, tofu and sausage meat wrapped in rice paper, a salad of cucumber and unidentified greens and tea for eighty-five cents.

Afterwards I walked over a curved bridge to an island in a lake where more birds and animals were kept in cages among gardens and under big trees. One strange triangular apparatus had four white long-haired cats in it. I wondered what they were but I couldn't read the label that described them. The zoo's toilet block was another of the topless open plan squat-on-the-tiles jobs. Its sewerage system was simplicity itself; an open drain ran straight outside into an open ditch.

The zoo was a long interesting cyclo ride from the centre of town. On the way I had passed the Hanoi Hilton, the grim gaol that was built by the French in the early twentieth century and was later used to house western prisoners of war. Situated in a pleasant commercial street, it came as a shock to see the building's barred windows and the barbed wire and glass shards on top of its surrounding wall.

Then we rode through the area of imposing houses and buildings that surrounds Ho Chi Minh's grey granite mausoleum. In Vietnam Uncle Ho is awarded the reverence due to, but seldom given, temples and deities. His tomb, set in a spacious square where no cars are admitted, looms over everything from the top of a massive set of steps. Inscribed over the entrance is Ho's quotation, 'Nothing is more precious than independence and freedom'. The Ho Chi Minh museum is opposite the mausoleum. It is a stupendous building that is also set up high for maximum impact and is approached by a mammoth flight of steps.

Extensive expanses of uncut lawns and acres of gardens intersected by paved paths surround the museum. I had walked to the far end of one of the paths when I was abruptly halted by a loud shouted, 'No!' This warning was uttered in an unmistakable tone by one of the many rifle-toting soldiers who patrolled the premises. I turned about smartly and went off in the other direction, but when I reached the end of that path I got the same reaction. I set off another way, this time escorted by four guards who had suddenly materialised to correct this erring foreigner. But they were friendly enough and when I said, 'Sorry' and laughed, they responded with jokes and we all marched along happily to the place permitted to Good Little Tourists.

In Vietnam I found what I had expected but did not get in China – oriental architecture and gardens in peaceful and serene surroundings. Van Mieu, the Temple of Literature in Hanoi, fulfilled all my expectations. It was the ultimate. The oldest school and the first university in the country, it was established in 1076 AD and dedicated to Confucius as a place of worship and learning. The entire complex was shut off from the noise of the street by high, thick walls that measured about a kilometre around. Only the faint murmur of traffic that seemed far away in another world reached inside this tranquil place where visitors were few and innumerable birds twittered in massive old trees. In the large grounds you could ramble on tree-shaded grass from courtyard to courtyard through ornate gateways. Each courtyard had a wooden pavilion in its centre and as you approached one courtyard you saw the pavilion of the next framed in its gateway, a beautiful, composed picture. At the rear of the complex grew the most ancient-looking tree that I have ever seen; a huge, gnarled and twisted frangipani that must have been hundreds of years old. A water puppet show was also staged at the back of the temple compound. The setting was a tank of flood-lit water and the puppets were manipulated from behind a screen as a story was told. The usual villain, hero and heroine were present and they were accompanied by boats and other water-craft. A fairy-land of magical illusion was created as the glittering reflections of the puppets, their colourful costumes and the sparkling lights moved on the water.

Another morning I was pedalled to the Viet Cong Bank. What a building! An enormous French colonial edifice, it had a ceiling thirty metres high that was inset with skylights of coloured glass and a series of curved staircases wound up to a lofty mezzanine floor. I crossed the marble floor that was edged by polished wooden couches and waited patiently in line for twenty minutes behind two Canadians who were trying to cash a traveller's cheque. Then I found that I was in the wrong queue.

When I left the bank, the Canadians were still trying to get their money, but a cash advance, and in American dollars, on my Visa Card had taken only a couple of minutes. You got much more value using US dollars than the local currency.

One evening I paid a call on the cathedral. A long central aisle led to a colourful main altar that was flanked by two minor ones. High above, the domed ceiling was shaped like a bishop's hat, and a wooden railed balcony in the rear housed the choir. I stepped soundlessly down the dusky aisle, my footsteps masked by rubber soles. The atmosphere was heavy with history. Ghosts lurked in the darkened, silent pews. I sat down to absorb the peace and quiet. Two or three people came in to pray. Then others began filtering in for evensong, mostly old women who wore heavy French head-dresses or scarves. I looked at their tranquil faces and wondered what they had lived through to have achieved this serenity. One smiled softly at me. The priest had a shock of white hair and was also old, almost in his dotage. He doddled around the altar on faltering feet, and when he came to a step the altar boy took his hand and helped him down. Incense burned, bells tinkled and candles flickered mystically. The choir and the old ladies raised their voices sweetly and the pure notes drifted away into the dim recesses of the vaulted ceiling.

On the steps outside the cathedral a legless beggar leaned on his crutches and solicited alms. It was a fine evening so I walked back to the Trung through streets that were now calm after the hustle of the day.

I got the urge to interfere with nature again and bought some hair colour. Ever since my days in Saudi Arabia when I could hide my mistakes under a veil I decide now and then to play with my hair – usually with disastrous results. I never learn! This time was no different. It was the usual debacle. My natural dark brown was stripped to a dull, dirty stripey blonde. I should have guessed when I saw the bottle labelled 'peroxide'. At least they called a spade a shovel here and didn't disguise it with euphemisms like activator or developer. But I was mystified how a bottle of liquid could produce stripes of a nasty green colour, like the shade you get when meat is turning bad, in your hair.

On my last day in Hanoi I visited Lenin Park. Written Le Nin, it is a big green area where large old flame trees, bamboos and palms flourish and iron and stone trellises are covered with bright, purple and pink flowering creepers. Fronting an extensive, glistening lake and garlanded by vines, rows of Grecian columns form walkways that look like scenes from Parish prints of the twenties. At the edge of the lake fishermen pulled in gigantic nets that had been set in a semi-circle and in which many small fish were entangled. They threw most of the fish back into the water, but two women gleaned those that fell from the edges of the nets, collected them in rattan baskets and bicycled away. From the amount of fish I saw jumping all over the water as the net was pulled in, the lake must have been teeming with fish. It was also teeming with rubbish.

But there was not much pollution. The air in Hanoi was clear. This was another perfect day for park meandering, sitting on benches along the stone walkways, or leaning on paved bridges. It was Saturday and lovers had commandeered many of the seats. Women vendors sold drinks from panniers on their bicycles and kids called out to me, 'Madame, Madame'. It was a restful place and no one hassled me. The children only came with wide smiles to say hello. A sweeper pulled a cart past me, with a forty-four gallon drum rubbish bin attached. Another cart was the water chariot and from it women gave the flower pots and urns their rations with a dipper and sprinkled the garden beds with galvanised-iron watering cans. A woman went by with all the ingredients for chewing betel nut in two baskets on her shoulder pole. I had seen betel juice on the ground, but chewing it did not seem to be a common practice in the cities although I did see old women doing this. Groups of men squatted on the grass playing cards or checkers and now and then I came across a man who had tied a hammock between two trees so that he could swing gently to and fro while gazing out over the lake. This looked a blissful occupation.

Returning from the park on foot, I was confronted by a street vendor who insisted on trying to sell me a live duck.

After staying ten days at the Trung, I took the train to Danang. When I went to pay my bill, I discovered that it had grown very big! I was given a calculator to add it up myself, but the sum I arrived at was not checked by Madame Doctor – even though I pleaded partial numerical illiteracy and begged her to. Doctor Marie (whom everyone, staff included, called Mumsy) just smiled and said, 'No problem.' I tried to pay for my laundry, but I was told to forget it, as well as the last lot of food and drink I'd had there. I was soundly kissed goodbye by everyone, especially Tham, the little worker who continually hummed, whistled or sang and always seemed happy and full of innocent fun.

I'd had some photocopying done in a shop near the Trung. The staff could not change the bank note I offered them, so they told me to come back later and pay, or forget it. I could suit myself. I don't believe this place, I thought as I regretfully left.

11 Chariots of Dire

Riding the Thong Nhat, The Vietnamese Unification Express, on a one-track, narrow gauge line is a bone rattling adventure. There are unscheduled stops and a good chance of derailment owing to flooding or typhoons, in the fifty-six hours it takes to reach Ho Chi Minh City. But it is one of the most spectacular train journeys in Asia. The train passes through a dramatic landscape of jagged granite mountains and rocky coastlines that is interrupted by long, coal black tunnels. Begun in 1899, the train-line was repeatedly sabotaged and bombed in the second world war, the Indochinese War and the American war and it was only re-opened in 1976.

Vietnamese trains are old, but they have been well cared for. I thought The Unification Express was wonderful. It was not as plush as the showcase Shanghai–Beijing train, but it was clean, including the loo, which even ran to the luxury of toilet paper. And the trains came with service with a smile. When I boarded at seven in the evening a conductor carried my bags on for me.

My two person compartment had an upper and lower berth and a wooden wash-stand in one corner, the lid of which lifted to disclose a small blue porcelain sink with a tap. Attached to the wall beside the wash-stand was a little fold-down table, beneath which nestled two tiny stools and a waste bin. It was a long time since I had seen one of those articles on a train. There were also bed lights, a fan and, apart from the outside windows, a window covered by an ornate, wrought-iron grill and a curtain that opened into the corridor.

The other half of the two-person cabin arrived; an interesting Englishman who was a steam railway buff. Nigel had some great train stories. We sat on the lower bunk talking for hours and soon became mates. After a while we were brought a plastic bag of long, stringy green tea and later still our minute table was ceremoniously laid with pepper, salt and toothpicks. But although we waited a very long time, nothing in the food line eventuated and regrettably we had nothing to pick out of our teeth. I think we had been expected to buy our dinner from a trolley that we unsuspectingly allowed to get past us. Breakfast, however, was delivered to us in bed – banana, noodles and meat, along with propaganda over the loudspeaker which started at half past five in the morning.

Nigel got off the train at nine o'clock in Hue. From there the line ran down the sea coast to Danang, three and a half hours away. The countryside was as lovely as I have seen anywhere. Buffalo stood among lush green trees and ducks puddled in wet rice paddies alongside thatched atap and bamboo, or occasionally a stone, house. Women stooped to work in the large expanses of fields in which bananas, sugar cane and vegetables grew in verdant profusion. In each rice paddy the tombs of its previous owners stood guard; the ancestor still looking over his rice. (Or had he been used as fertiliser?) The red, blue and yellow of the painted head stones had been faded by the weather, which gave them added charm. The occasional paddy accommodated a veritable cemetery of tombs, some of which were quite large and contained a stone sarcophagus. Reminders of the American War, bomb craters were visible alongside bridges and riverbanks. We crossed several big rivers on which narrow boats bobbed, while on the banks men fished and women washed their clothes. At a little town made up of a motley collection of low buildings that were mostly stone, I noticed that spirit houses decorated with offerings stood on posts in front of all the dwellings. The red Vietnamese flag flew above the railway station. Its doors had once been painted bright blue, but were now attractively weathered to a more subtle colour. As we crossed more rivers, I began to realise just how much water there is in this country.

The railway line began to follow a line of blue mountain peaks on one side, while on the other, waves beat on the white sand of the shore. Then we were among mountains so skyscraping that smoke-like cloud wreathed their tops. We had reached the majestically beautiful Hai Van, The Pass of The Clouds, where the mountains plummet dramatically straight into the sea. We went through several long tunnels that had been cut through the mountains and a guard with a red flag and a whistle stopped the train in a village high on a mountain. From my window I looked down into a deep crevice that was completely overgrown with luxuriant vegetation that cascaded all the way to where the sea swept around the coast in dramatic curves. From this height it was a spectacular sight. The train emerged from the final tunnel to run along the outer edge of a towering, jungle covered cliff. Far below, the sea crashed in waves over black rocks, smashing itself into swirling, foaming white water while the rushing water of small streams tumbled down the mountains over smooth stones and boulders to join it.

At Danang the conductor helped me off the train. Smiling, he happily carried my bags as though it was his duty and not as though he was doing me a favour. As I left the station, I was accosted by several touts, who, though not aggressive, insisted that I should take a taxi to Hoian. I said, 'No, cyclo to bus station.' A cyclo was produced, but one bloke, who was still determined to taxi me to Hoian, rode alongside it on his motorbike. When he couldn't convince me to take a taxi, he said that he would take me on the motorbike. I said, 'No no,' and pointed to my luggage. 'No problem,' he insisted. Maybe not for him, but I wasn't bumping thirty kilometres over bad roads on the back of a motorbike clutching my luggage. Still trying to persuade me, he said, 'Vietnamese bus very old.' I said I didn't mind,

'Vietnamese bus very crowded.'

Ditto.

'Vietnamese bus no good.'

Ditto.

'There will be Vietnamese people on this bus.'

'I love Vietnamese people.' I laughed.

'There will be *many* Vietnamese people.'

'The more the merrier!' I chortled.

I won. He gave up.

'Ever onwards!' I enthused, pointing, I hoped, in the direction of the bus station with my trusty umbrella. But when the cyclo and my entourage deposited me at the station, I began to see their point. At the bus station I found, not real buses, but a yard full of senile four-wheel-drive wrecks that appeared to have been hashed up out of scrap metal. Built high off the ground, they resembled a mistake between a small truck and a van that had been badly converted into a passenger vehicle by shoving bench seats in the back. I was allotted pride of place in the front seat – possibly because I had paid twenty times the local price, even after bargaining the fare down to half the starting point. My bags and I were pushed into the vehicle to rest on a rock-hard bench that was so high I had to duck my head to see out of the windscreen. Not having a death wish, I always try to steer away from the front seat of anything drivable in Asia, but somehow I usually manage to end up there anyway. I am not tired of living just yet and if the vehicle I am in is about to have a horror smash, I really don't want to see it coming at me head on. But in this instance I need not have worried. The broken-down conveyance wobbled along, crashing through its gears, sounding like a sick food processor. It could not have gone fast enough to have had a decent smash.

The driver climbed in. Instead of one of the young macho boys, who look about ten years old, smoke full time and drive like loonies, that are usually found in charge of public transport in South East Asia, in creaked a tiny, wizened-up geriatric, who looked as though he should have been licensed to drive a wheel chair, at the very most. He gave me a huge, almost toothless grin, and was obviously delighted to see me. I sat hunched almost double on the bench. My big bag was crushed between the Wizened One and me, the smaller one was under my feet and my handbag was stuck up in front of me on the dashboard like an object of worship. As we took off, I looked down at the door by my side and saw a hand creep around to secure the latch on the inside of the door. The kind gentleman in the seat behind me obviously did not want to see me bite the dust. Then I discovered that this door failed to meet the frame by about an inch and that the bolt which had been banged on as an after thought was extremely insecure. Expecting to fall out at any second, I rode clinging to the seat and the dash board with my fingernails.

We doddled along very slowly over an appalling dirt road that I thought was crook until we turned off it and I discovered that it had been the main road. Now we were on a track of rocks, pot holes, ditches and mud – it had been raining here. We crashed over this monstrosity at about one kilometre an hour for what seemed a very long time. It took an hour and a half to go thirty kilometres. Touting for extra passengers, we stopped every now and then and more people, lots of live chooks, ducks and a pig or two, joined our group.

Advancing through rice paddies and vegetable gardens, we came to the sea shore, which we followed. We passed the turn off to China Beach, and finally came to the outskirts of

Hoian. An ancient town on the banks of the River Thu Bon, which winds down to the China Sea, Hoian was once one of the biggest ports in Asia. It is a rich fusion of Chinese, Japanese, Vietnamese and European influences, the latter dating back to the sixteenth century. In its earliest days, around the year 2 AD, the town was a port of the Champa kingdom and its annual spring fair grew to be an exotic showcase of the world's goods – silks, brocades, ivory, fragrant oils and fine porcelain. The now drowsy river was once thronged with majestic vessels that came with the trade winds from the great merchant nations of the world. But the river started to silt up in the late eighteenth century and Hoian's fortunes began to decline.

From its fringes, Hoian looked like a simple village, and I wondered if I had come to the wrong place. This was on the cards. But I knew all was well when I asked a cyclo driver to take me to the Hoian Hotel and he good-naturedly agreed. According to the guidebook, the Hoian Hotel was the only place that was permitted to take foreigners. But the book was outdated. All the small guest houses were now allowed to house foreigners and the place was jumping with them. I reflected sadly that Vietnam would soon become another Bali. Many of the foreigners were ghastly package tour monstrosities. One bunch of Italian men careered around in a screech of loud, lairy check-patterned shorts and plastic sandals and behaved like complete yobbos. Suffering from herd mentality, they went everywhere *en masse* in crocodile file. Obviously believing that they needed the safety of numbers, they trooped out in line to shop, tramping into one place after another, and making complete exhibitions of themselves in each.

The cyclo pedalled me along the wide drive that swept up to the main entrance of the Hoian Hotel – the only place in town that looked as though it was accustomed to its guests arriving in cars. You didn't see many cars in Hoian, but this was where they were to be found. I imagined that respectable tourists did not land here in cyclos. The Hoian complex was very extensive and I discovered that I had got out at the restaurant by mistake. A girl took me in tow and walked me through the vast grounds.

At the reception desk I was told that the Hoian had several grades of accommodation, and I negotiated for one of the cheaper rooms. Two people travelling together can afford better rooms, but when you have to pay the lot yourself it is not practical. Another young woman walked me across more of the grounds to show me the room. I had become cautious when she had said that it had an outside bathroom. I had been caught in this trap before.

The Hoian had been the original old pub in French colonial days, but it was now run by the government. I was billeted in the oldest part, which was now the poor quarters. It consisted of several antiquated, but charming bungalows that fronted the street and were some distance from the main hotel building. Each bungalow had four very large rooms and was surrounded by a wide tiled verandah supported by stone columns. Colourful decorated pots containing plants, trees and palms flanked the steps up to the verandahs.

The first room I viewed did have an outside bathroom. You had to walk across the verandah, step off it, go along the side of the building and enter an old wooden door. My accomplice and I looked at this arrangement with a jaundiced eye. She said, 'No, you have other room.' This one's bathroom was more convenient. A door at the end of the room opened into a corridor right next to one, albeit with only cold water.

The main Hoian Hotel was a white-washed building with a tiled roof and wide verandahs. It reminded me of the old Dutch hotels in Indonesia. During the American War it had accommodated the US marines. The grounds were surrounded by a stone wall broached by a gate at the street front. A guard was stationed here who watched all entries and exits from a small hut under a pink hibiscus tree.

My room was comfortable and I circumvented the lack of hot water by using the thermoses provided. The room attendants were quite happy to replenish them often, and they also asked if I wanted anything else. The weather was not as cold as it had been in Hanoi, and nothing like the freezing conditions I had survived in China, and I had already learned to wash my hair in a thermos of water and perform my ablutions with a little less.

The side wall of my room had two big windows which opened only a couple of feet from the main street. They were covered by wooden shutters, fancy wrought-iron grilles, cotton curtains and even pelmets, but they had no glass. Someone, the window fairy or the Malaria Police, closed the shutters at dusk to keep the mosquitoes out. Double doors led in from the verandah. The walls were wood panelled up to head height all the way around. The ceiling was also wooden and from it rotated an overhead fan. The floor was covered with green floral tiles and I was given enormous plastic shoes to walk on them – obviously footwear designed for men. They were huge on me.

The Hotel Rules were better than the comics: 'No bicycles motor bikes animals and even prostitutes explosives stinking inflammable things not allowed in room. Please respest local custom bare legs arms shoulders not polite.'

Having established myself and arranged the room to suit me, I had a rest. Restored, I went for a walk. Hoian was easy to get around on foot. Once you left the three main streets parallel with the river that were the core of the town, you were in paved lanes that were only accessible to foot traffic anyway. The town meanders along the banks of the river and so did I, walking alongside it on a road that was fringed with red flowering flame trees. Many sampans, some waiting for customers to ferry across the water, were moored along the river's edge. Very old, wood and stone houses with moss-covered tiled roofs and wooden shutters, and wooden-fronted shop houses lined the narrow streets of this amiable town. Fortunately most of Hoian escaped damage in the American and second world wars. I saw one house that had a lean-to which must have been the wash-house attached to its front – a copper boiled on a wood fire beside it.

Cows wandered freely through the streets of Hoian, leaving the evidence of their passing that had to be avoided when walking. Lumbering bullock carts also rolled through the town, but hand carts that were pushed and pulled by people-power seemed to be the way that most goods were moved. I saw an inordinate amount of shops that sold only herbs and medicines. The Vietnamese seemed to be as addicted to self prescription as the Chinese.

I was happy to discover that Hoian had plenty of good, small cafés with extremely cheap food and English menus. Even if they were ambiguous at times, the menus at least gave you an idea of what you were likely to be offered. Sometimes, however, something in your interpretation or theirs was lost and the dish turned out to be a novel experience. At Lilly Lye's café in the main street, I had a great meal of rice, eggs and meat with delicious, hot, fresh-squeezed lemonade – the cheapest drink you could buy here, apart from tea – followed by frozen yoghurt mixed with strawberry jam, peanuts and chocolate. It all cost about a dollar.

Later I walked to the end of the street where an immense covered market was in full swing. At its front, under tarpaulins and with mud underfoot, were the vegetable, produce and fruit stalls. I asked a woman for bananas. She didn't have any. Taking me firmly by the wrist, she trundled me around the market until she found someone who did. Then she waited to see that I made a good transaction before we parted.

Further on, the street was lined with touristy shops that offered much antique porcelain, mostly blue and white Chinese or Vietnamese of the Ming and Ching dynasties. Sadly, it was poor-quality stuff that had been made for the export market and a great deal of it appeared to have been buried, or immersed in water, and was almost worthless. There were also a lot of fakes or, more politely, recent reproductions. The main street also contained several shops where gold jewellery was sold by weight and was cheap at eleven American dollars a gram.

One day I watched from Lilly's café as an old woman set up her rival portable restaurant on the pavement opposite. She trotted up with two baskets on her shoulder poles in which reposed the entire dining establishment. Under a rickety piece of straw matting that was held up by two crooked bamboo poles attached to the wall, she laid out her stock in trade, arranged three tiny stools and was in business, cooking and serving on the ground. At night she went more upmarket and produced a low table, more stools and a lantern. There were always customers by her side. Nobody seemed to eat at home. Small cafés and portable stalls lit by lamps and candles were dotted all along the streets at night.

The next morning was overcast but not cold. I breakfasted at Lilly Lye's café on omelette, hot lemon and French toast. From the footpath of the café, I watched two little old nuns dressed in pale grey *ao dais* and straw conical hats, toddle down the street holding each other by the hand. They were followed by a bevy of beautiful teenage students, immaculate in spotless, white flowing *ao dais* carrying their books to school. Nurses and female doctors dressed in white also passed en route to the hospital. The *ao dais*, the national costume, has graceful lines that suit the slim figures of Vietnamese women. It consists of soft material made into wide-legged, white or black trousers that are topped by a fitted tunic that flows out from the hips, and high heeled sandals called *guoc*.

I walked about all day enjoying this lovely antiquated town. I was back in 'You are very beautiful' territory and was told this frequently. I knew it was only my novelty value and a good paint job, but I can still take a lot of it. In what was previously the French Quarter, one family invited me into their house as I went by. We sat on the balcony and they gave me strong black coffee and pieces of dried, sugared coconut.

In the market I tried to buy a new light bulb for my emergency lighting kit. Even though I took the broken one along as a sample, I had no joy. I was wandering off when a young girl from a stall I had enquired at caught up with me. Taking me by the hand, she dragged me behind her through the maze of stalls to a shop that sold electrical items where the defunct bulb was exchanged for a functioning model.

Across from my hotel room I found a small tourist operator. Well, he actually found me, he practically hijacked me off the street, but he did it so agreeably that I did not mind. Mr Nuygen helped me buy a train ticket to Natrang, a reputedly lovely beach resort. When I looked at my receipt, I saw that it was a plain sheet of paper with an amount of money written on it. Underneath, he had added, 'You've paid enough money.'

I had wanted to go back to Danang by river and sea, which I knew was possible, but the only way I could do this was to hire a boat all to myself, and the cost was exorbitant.

The charming tour operator then asked me if I'd like to see the local pottery factory which was ten kilometres away on a dirt road. We negotiated a price for me to ride pillion on his motorbike. As soon as I climbed aboard the motorbike, it started to drizzle and by the time we returned it was pelting down. I looked like a drowned rat. But the ride had been worth it. We bumped through a series of small cheery villages that edged the river. The hard-packed earth around them was swept immaculately clean and palm and banana trees, greenery and plants in pots separated the small houses. Approaching the tiny potting village, brick kiln after brick kiln and heaps and heaps of bricks announced their trade. All the bricks for the district were made here from local clay. As my friend manoeuvred his bike along diminutive lanes to worm our way deep into the depths of the village, the bike's handlebars grazed the walls of the close-set houses and now and then clean and contented pigs grunted and snuffled at me from little bamboo styes.

The potters were a toothless old mother and her middle-aged daughter. The latter worked squatting on the ground, while the old woman stood and operated the potting wheel with one foot, swinging her leg rhythmically across it and not working a pedal as was usual. The potting was very skilful, but the small figurines and pots they made were only fired in the biscuit and not glazed. Children – and such beautiful children – crept up in ones and twos until I counted nine of them standing in a row before me, drinking me in, highly entertained.

Then it was back on the motorbike. I paused to think, Could this be me? I, who had sworn never to set foot on one of these Chariots of Dire unless it was with someone who was at the very least a blood relative and certainly never in Asia? Not only because the risk of an accident was high, but because of what happened to you in Asian hospitals!

Hoian's delightful post office was only a short walk from my hotel. It was the most comfortable old post office I have ever seen. Decorative urns containing ficus trees flanked the entrance door to welcome you. Inside four carved wooden armchairs with finials and knobbly legs – just like mine – had been placed convivially around a wooden table on a ceramic tiled floor. A carved bench, partitioned into four sections so that the people next to you couldn't see what you were writing was in front of that. The furniture was the same as the Trung's in Hanoi – a hybrid of oriental and European styles. The walls were decorated with imitation flowers and real hanging green plants and in one corner there was even a basin where you could wash your hands. The two telephone booths were fitted out with a chair, an electric fan and a vase of plastic flowers for you to contemplate while chatting. But there were IDD facilities, and a computer-operated phone that told you how long you had spoken. You could even buy a toothbrush here, if you should get the urge for one while making a phonecall. They were displayed under glass-topped counters along with the postcards and envelopes.

The post office staff were friendly and accommodating. By now I was becoming blase about this again. Two tiny girls about six years old helped me post my card and then stood, one at either of my shoulders, when I sat down to look at the pack of local postcards that I had just bought. The little ones gave each other a delighted commentary, exclaiming excitedly as they recognised each place. A third small girl sat quietly in the chair opposite me, saucer eyed, absorbing me. She seemed particularly fascinated with my feet. Finally she leaned forward and ever so gently passed one of her little fingers back and forth across my ankle. I realised then that she had never seen panty-hose before. She smiled up at me and when I did not bite her, greatly daring, she picked up a piece of the material between her finger and thumb and rubbed it. A look of sheer rapture came over her face. Her little friends joined her in this occupation. Wow! she seemed to say to them. Look at this! They peeped at each other and tittered, then excitedly discussed this phenomenon.

In one of the main streets of the town, I found the 200-year-old former home of a Chinese merchant that had been faithfully preserved as a shrine for ancestor worship. Tan Ky house, in which the merchant's family still lived, lay behind a massive old stone wall that enclosed a typically oriental garden. The house was wonderful. Approached through a gateway covered by a stone arch, it was a combination of Javanese, Chinese and Vietnamese styles and material that the merchant had acquired in his travels. It was constructed entirely of wood, most of which was heavily carved. Huge columns made from whole Javanese trees supported the roof and rafters and beams crossed the wooden ceilings and overhanging verandah. There were no interior walls, only carved wooden screens that were fenestrated on the top half to allow the breeze through. A large ornate altar held pride of place in the main room. It was decorated with hefty, 200-year-old blue and white Chinese jars and delicate bowls that held the daily offerings of fruit, rice and flowers. Flickering candles and burning joss sticks had been placed before photos of some of the ancestors. Before photos were available, wooden boxes inscribed outside with the ancestor's name and containing his CV and some personal memento, such as his seal, were placed on the altar.

The present owner of the house was the original merchant's great-great-grandson. A gracious man, he offered me a chair and served me home-made lotus flower tea and delicious dried coconut snacks while he told me the history of his house. Explaining ancestor worship, Tan Jai said that the Vietnamese worship their ancestors inside their houses, but are Buddhists outside. The outside god does not come inside the house, he said.

There were many attractive pieces of antique porcelain in the house, and in a back room, I was shown the porcelain collection I had heard about. Some of it was for sale, but most of it had been recovered from a sunken ship and was water damaged; some pieces even had sea shells stuck to them. Unfortunately, only a few of the bigger bowls were worth buying, and they were too heavy to be a practical consideration. They were also expensive, but Tan Jai told me that up until two years ago they would have sold for a mere couple of dollars. The story of my life. Now it was too late.

I visited the Fuk I En temple. Outside it old ladies sat selling incense and candles. I had been surprised to find how active religion was in Vietnam and how many private homes and shops contained altars, or had spirit houses in front of them. When I asked what people had done during the hard-line communist rule, I was told that religion had remained alive but had become clandestine. Near the temple is an extremely archaic-looking, Japanese covered bridge which was known to exist in the sixteenth century. It is said to have been built by the Japanese community in order to link them to the Chinese across the creek.

Three mornings later it was still raining. Winter had now arrived. Everything was damp and my clothes wouldn't dry. Down the street strode a loud, but very bad, drum band of young boys in uniform. They were followed by lines of marching high school kids. Behind them there was a van that bore a huge sign warning against the dangers of AIDS, and a megaphone on its roof blared out a harangue. I sat on my balcony and wrote postcards to send for Christmas until it stopped raining. Then I went out without my umbrella. Murphy waited until I was well away and then arranged for it to pour, and I was forced to buy a purple mushroom rain-cape like everyone in South Indo-China seemed to have. I felt like a well-wrapped parcel in it, but at least I was dry.

That evening when I came out of my room in search of my dinner, I found that the rain had stopped, but all the lights in town had gone out. The only dim flickerings around the streets came from little kerosene lamps. I had noticed many of them for sale in the market and I had soon learned why. The power failed in Hoian with monotonous regularity. It had gone off every day since I had arrived, sometimes for hours, even in the Hoian hotel which had its own generator.

I stumbled along the rutted roads and footpaths in absolute darkness. Unlit bicycles whizzed past me. They hardly ever had lights. I was eating at a café when a real tropical rain began pelting down in earnest and my table under the verandah on the footpath became so wet I had to move inside. I loved the rain, but I had to wade and paddle home through running water in the dark; the power still had not come back on.

In the cafés I frequented I met two people I had encountered previously in Hanoi, as well as my erstwhile train companion, Nigel. And a new friend, who had hired a car and driver to come to Hoian for two days and with whom I arranged to share a ride back to Danang. It was extraordinary how you caught up with the same people when travelling. John, the Englishman I had travelled with from Yanshu to Guangzhou, had turned up in the Trung guest house in Hanoi on the same night that I had. Yet when we had parted in Guangzhou, he had been going down to Thailand via Hong Kong and I was supposedly going home.

The next day it was still raining and it looked like continuing to do so for some time. I sat in the middle of the river – in what was called a floating restaurant, but was really a café on a ramshackle pontoon – watching the rain that hadn't let up for three days. But my father had taught me that I should never complain about rain, only the lack of it. The restaurant, a wooden edifice that resembled a pagoda, was reached on a wooden bridge from the riverbank. It was surrounded by verandahs, awnings, wooden balconies and railings that had plants in pots secured to their outside edges and made me feel rather as though I was on a wet floating garden.

The next day, when I drove to Danang with the young Frenchman I had met in Lilly's café, it was still pouring with rain.

12 Tin Pan Alley

At Danang railway station I bought a ticket for the nine-hour ride to Natrang, a seaside town halfway down the coast to the capital, Ho Chi Minh City. I was the only foreigner in the train's first-class carriage. The seats were old-fashioned recliners and from the back of the one in front a small tray could be pulled down. This augured well for food, I thought. Sure enough, soon a trolley was pulled through the carriage and I was offered drinks and nibbles. Luggage was stored in large lockers of white laminex that hung overhead and the latest addition to this 1950s train was a video screen that had been suspended in a similar box in the middle of the carriage. It was, of course, showing blood-thirsty horrors. The original sound-track was in English, but instead of being dubbed the film had an 'explainer', who told the story over the actors' voices. This proved frustrating as I could still almost, but not quite, hear them. The sound track of the second film was simply drowned by a Vietnamese song that was played loudly over and over. At first I thought that the lovely tune was the theme song of the film, but then I twigged that what was obviously a sweet and charming love song was incompatible with the murder and carnage that was taking place on the screen. The actors were wrecking mayhem on each other; chopping off heads with swords, kicking each other to death and generally being thoroughly unpleasant.

I turned my attention to the green and silver land outside

the train. Mile after mile of it followed; rice paddies overlaid with water, fields of bamboo, sugar cane and bananas and countless rivers, all viewed through a shimmering veil of slanting rain. When we came to villages, some of which were made up of thatched hovels, others of small stone buildings, the train guard put a yellow or red flag out of the window and a guard at the station we were passing through would respond with the same.

They fed us dinner with the chooks. The conductors brought around meals on a trolley at half past four. The food was set out in a compartmented plastic tray; a big space for rice, a slot for meat, another for vegetables and a special little groove shaped exactly to fit one fresh chilli. There was also a bowl of cabbage soup which I used to moisten the dry rice. The pepper and roughly ground sea salt came already mixed in a tiny plastic tub and two tooth picks were supplied. They had ends as blunt as fence posts that you had to chew to get a point. I was also given a free can of soft drink. As I had paid one hundred per cent extra for my ticket, I suppose this was fair enough.

Dark came early. By half past five dusk was gathering on the calmness over the rice paddies. Their waters changed from silver to gun-metal and then they were no more. Now all I saw were a few small yellow glows that suggested a village among the trees. The rain continued and I decided not to get off at Natrang, but to go on to Ho Chi Minh City. It would have been a bit of a fizz to visit a beautiful beach resort in a pouring deluge. The train only stopped once before Natrang. More passengers got on and I discovered that I was in someone else's seat. But there were spare seats so we sorted it out amicably.

As this stop had been the last place that passengers would be boarding the train, I decided to try my luck at getting a sleeper. I waved my ticket at the conductor and he seemed to understand. He went away and returned shortly with an

English speaking railway worker, who sat beside me and talked for a while, telling me about his daughter who lived in Sydney. After a time he also went away, but came back later saying, 'You come with me. I will show you what you can have.' He led me to a four berth compartment full of men who were smoking up a storm. I said, 'Heavens! I don't want that. I'd rather sit up all night than be locked in there with all that smoke.'

The conductor explained hastily that the men were only train employees, who were taking advantage of the empty compartment for a little relaxation and that they would be turfed out if I took up residence. We agreed upon a price. I was sure that some of it went into the conductor's pocket, but I like to support private enterprise. In Hoian another traveller had told me that he had tried to change from a seat to a sleeper on this train but had been told that it could not be done. Fortunately I never believe the first thing I am told. I have found that although sometimes you cannot do the things that are said to be possible, depending on your approach, you can often do things that have been declared impossible.

Safely installed in the incredibly freezing airconditioning of the compartment, I settled down for the night, glad that I had kept a few woollies when I left Hoian for the anticipated warmth of the south.

The compartment door had no lock, so I tied it shut with one of my socks, which turned out to be a good idea as about fifteen people tried to get in with me during the night. Maybe they were checking to see if I was all right, or if I was behaving myself. I did not care. The sock kept them out.

When we stopped at Natrang at half past ten, it was still raining and I was glad that I had decided to continue on south. We arrived in Ho Chi Minh City at seven the next morning. I took a cyclo to a small hotel that was not in the guidebook, but which a New Zealand couple I had met in

Hanoi had recommended and marked on my map. I was greeted enthusiastically by an agreeable man who made me feel very much at home. He brought me coffee and a terrific breakfast of eggs and bread accompanied by what he regarded as suitable eating equipment for a foreigner – a knife and fork. The fork was one of those diabolical instruments they produce in Asia which have prongs that are cut off square and have no points, and the knife was a bread knife – a huge, bone-handled affair. I would have been better off with chopsticks.

While I wrestled with my breakfast, my new friend told me that he had been a captain in the army – unfortunately for him, on the side that lost the war, and he had subsequently spent four years in prison after it ended.

The hotel owner drifted downstairs to inspect me. Looking like a Lady of the Night in a pair of short black frilly silk pyjamas, she swanned about in the foyer which was completely open to the street. In the full light of day this looked a bit strange. It also seemed odd that at night, although the hotel was full and there was no need to attract more guests, a small counter was set up on the steps outside the front door. Here, right on the street, Madame, with her once beautiful face, sat jangling her dozens of wide gold bangles.

My room was a passageway that had been partitioned into a makeshift, windowless cubicle by a simple piece of gash engineering. The wall, which had previously finished at head height, had been extended to the ceiling by the addition of a piece of lattice that had had opaque plastic stapled over it in a most haphazard manner. The furniture comprised a bed and an intriguing, waist-high cupboard that had been constructed from the same kind of white enamel that panikins and mugs are made of. There was an extremely wobbly wall fan and a table lamp on the cupboard provided the only illumination. The electricity supply for these two items came in over the flimsy door on a dubious-looking extension cord and power-board. Every time I walked past the light, it went out!

The 'en suite' bathroom was almost outside. It was another piece of corridor that had been partitioned off next to my room. I entered it by a door screened with a curtain which continuously fell down. The hand basin had been inadequately waterproofed with a layer of thick, uneven grout and it piddled profusely on my feet whenever I used it. But the staff, who consisted of Madame, the Officer and Gentleman and a Boy, were extremely kind and solicitous of my safety. Every time I went out they worried for me, telling me that I would get 'stolen'. Was there much of a market for second-hand ladies who were ever so slightly over the hill, I wondered? And each time when, to their surprise, I returned safely to the hotel, they greeted me like the prodigal child returning.

Saigon, (the locals still call the town Saigon, as this remains the name of the main downtown district) 1700 kilometres due south of Hanoi, has a population of four million and is situated on the Saigon River, forty kilometres above the fertile Mekong Delta. Originally a sleepy Cambodian Khymer fishing backwater and trading post in the sixth century, it was the seaport of the Kingdom of Angkor Cambodia in the eleventh and twelfth centuries. The town fell into Vietnamese hands in the seventeenth century, and was re-built as a colonial city in 1859 by the French, who named it Saigon, 'Wood of the Kapok Tree', and made it the pearl of the Orient.

The first night I spent in Saigon there was the grand-mother of all thunderstorms. It was wonderful. I love a real tropical commotion. There was thunder, lightning and torrents of rain that bucketed down in great sheets. It was more satisfying to watch than to go out in, however, especially at night. But it was dinnertime and I was hungry, so I braved the deluge and the dark. Putting on my purple plastic cape and raising my pink brolly, I sloshed down the street and around the corner to Kym's café, a well known travellers' hangout.

Feeling like some western food I ordered 'mashed pottatos and meat souse' and wondered what on earth would appear. To my delight, I was presented with a marvellous big pile of proper mashed potatoes that were covered with a good, thick bolognaise sauce.

At Kym's I met an Australian called Angela who was on her way to Europe to visit her relatives. She was working her way through the cocktail menu and, having made the halfway mark, was in good form. Cocktails cost 5000 dong, fifty cents, and were delicious mixes of lovely, tasty freshly squeezed fruit juices and the tasty, but unlovely fresh squeezed local jungle juice or fire water. The drinks were listed as pina colada, screwdriver, etc. but the alcohol content was always the same – potent. The Australian miss was getting very sloshed. Not that daring, I had a bottle of the local beer.

In the morning I set off on foot in search of a bank. I got lost and never found the one I had been directed to by the hotel staff. I think I went in the opposite direction. Banks were one of my favourite places for a rest. They were cool, comfy and elegant and apart from couches and armchairs they provided high-backed bar stools at the counter. In one bank I watched a workman cleaning the iron grills and railing on the outside ledge of the mezzanine floor high above. He had a thick rope tied around his middle as security against a fall. I am no judge of distance, but it was obvious to me that the rope was longer than the drop to the floor.

All the reports I'd had about Saigon were that it was incredibly hot. But I found that the weather was sticky but not unbearable. As I walked about I could not help noticing that many homeless people were living in the streets. Many looked desperate, and some accosted me for money. The streets were also a place of business for many itinerant vendors. There were toy cars, bikes, aeroplanes and trains made from used Coke cans and hats that had been fashioned from packing foam and old cardboard boxes. Vietnam is one of the poorest countries in the world, but its economy, which was lately in chaos, is slowly reviving.

I returned to the hotel by cyclo, clutching a coconut that I had bought from a street vendor. The top of the coconut had been struck off on the spot with a murderous looking machete and I had been given a straw with which to drink the milk. It was palatable and refreshing and, despite the heat of the day, was as cold as if it had been refrigerated. At the hotel the staff and I sat in the foyer and demolished the coconut flesh.

Angela, the Australian I had met in Kym's, had told me about the guest-house where she was staying. It sounded much better than my hotel and it was half the price – with breakfast. I went to check it out, got lost, but found it eventually. It was hidden away in a maze of alleys that I would never have thought to look in if the local people had not directed me there. To reach it I had to turn off a small street into an alleyway between two buildings, then pass into another even tinier alley which was so narrow the houses almost touched overhead – you could step across from one balcony to another. The guest-house was one of those delightful, Lilliputian, but attenuated wedding cake affairs.

The room I was offered was brand new; I would be its first tenant. I could hardly believe that its price was a ridiculous five dollars. The only drawback was that the balcony around my room was still in production and several workmen were madly busy with noisy power tools. Vien, the young woman who was the dominant family member, said that the work would be finished today. It wasn't, of course. It was the

Asian way to promise you something that never eventuated but kept you happy at the time. The members of the extended family who lived in the house and took care of the guests were extraordinarily kind and generous, and practised true Asian hospitality. As soon as I arrived, Vien put a cold drink in front of me, and every time she got the chance she did the same again. The minute I sat down in the living room something appeared in front of me – fruit juice, Coke or sweet lady-finger bananas. It was almost an embarrassment that I was never charged for any of this extra generosity.

Vien insisted on giving me a ride back to my hotel on her motorbike. I leaped onto the back of her small machine and this young, slim girl, whom I later discovered to be thirty-eight and the mother of a whacking big teenager, zipped me adroitly in and out of the heavy traffic.

The news that I was leaving her was not received with delight by my present landlady. Madame looked peevish and told me that my new hotel was situated in a very bad place, that the people who lived there were an evil lot, and that I would come to no good end with them. I replied that although I liked Madame and her establishment very much, I liked the other place more.

Still, I had a few misgivings as I was cycloed through the close packed alleys to reach my new digs. I thought life could be rough and tough here. But as soon as I was installed in my big airy room my fears were allayed. I was to find in these alleys a view of the real life of Saigon. Here I was treated as a member of the family and I lived local life as opposed to being sequestered in a tourist or traveller's ghetto.

My room was cool, thanks to its smooth tiled floor, high ceilings and overhead fan. But a long window that ran across the top of one wall was uncurtained and I soon realised that it afforded a terrific view into my room from the balcony upstairs. When I mentioned it to Vien, she said, 'Yes yes yes, it will be fixed straight away.' Remarkably, when I returned the next afternoon, a green curtain had been added.

Tiles and terrazzo abounded in Vietnamese houses and all the work was done by hand. Eight men worked flat out for two days to create a terrazzo floor on the balcony outside my room. On the morning I moved in they were making such a deafening din that I took off for the rest of the day and did not return until after five, when I thought they would be finished. But they worked on until it was completely dark.

My room fronted the alley. Across the balcony behind it there was an uncompleted room used for storage. In its midst was a carved wooden bed and on its bare boards an old man with only one arm was fast asleep. In Vietnam I saw many people who were missing an arm, a leg, or bits thereof. On the wall above the bed was a shrine on which a red light shone constantly. I decided that this man, who was one of the uncles, was a mystic. Every night at dusk he would light incense and sit cross-legged on the bed under a mosquito net contemplating his altar.

My complimentary breakfast was served whenever I decided to appear in the downstairs rooms. Grandmother waited on me like an honoured guest, bringing me the eggs, bread and wonderful coffee I had requested, as well as a bonus of two bananas. The eggs were fried in coconut oil and were great and the warm bread rolls were divine. As I sat enjoying a leisurely second cup of coffee, Vien walked past carrying a posy of white daisies in a blue and white reproduction Ming vase. They were for my room, and in passing she told me that there would be a party tonight at seven o'clock and asked if I would come.

After breakfast Vien asked me where I was going and when I said, 'Downtown to the post office' she insisted on ferrying me there. I never thought I'd see the day (or the next one either, for that matter) that I would be riding, or rather, roaring, across downtown Saigon in peak-hour traffic on the back of a motorbike. I closed my eyes, hoped for the best, and arrived at the post office with my hair standing on end – and not just from the breeze.

Clinging on the pillion for grim death, I had watched motorbikes and cars coming at me from all angles. They followed no road rules. If people drove like that in Australia there would be constant prangs. Crossing the street was the same death-defying deed as it had been in China and I was once again advised that it was better not to stand still. You kept moving, but very slowly, so that bikes and motorbikes could avoid you. And, surprisingly, it worked – it's harder to hit a moving target. But it was hair-raising and in Saigon my hair stood up permanently.

The post office contained crowds of people, but it was so spacious that it didn't matter. A magnificent French building that had been built in 1883, with a towering domed ceiling and iron framework, its exterior was painted a mellow shade of ochre. The colour scheme inside the building was also pleasing: dark green with touches of a lighter green and dabs of old gold. Long rows of small, dark-green and old gold-edged windows lined the walls and graceful supporting columns rose from floor to ceiling or stood against the walls. Wrought-iron friezes were looped between the columns and from them hung decorative antique lights. A gigantic portrait of Uncle Ho gazed benevolently down from one wall onto the people below who rested on the comfortable wooden benches, or wrote at the desks. Envelopes, postcards and stamps were sold over wooden counters and there was even a special counter for posting foreign mail. It was such a serene place and so beautifully reminiscent of bygone days that I spent hours there. I could have taken up permanent residence quite happily.

A large open square dominated by an enormous white

statue of the Virgin Mary stood in front of the post office. On one side of the square was St Mary's Cathedral, a massive edifice built in 1877 in the style of Notre Dame. On the other was a little park that provided seats under tall tamarand trees. In many Asian cities there are no small parks, but in Saigon I frequently found grassy places to rest under trees. As this day was Sunday I decided to visit the cathedral. It did not have the ambience of Hanoi's cathedral but, apart from the odd bit of tacky coloured neon light, reminiscent of a nightclub entrance, over the altars, it was impressive. One side altar held a graceful statue of the virgin Mary that was made fantastically beautiful by the light of numerous softly glowing candles. Deciding to stay for a while in the cool gloom to listen to the choir singing, I did what I presumed to be the right thing and dropped to my knees. I got a terrific shock when I crashed onto the wooden floor. There was no kneeling board. Watching others coming in, I saw that they merely bowed to the altar and then sat down. I hoped that those who had witnessed my fall from grace would make allowances for my being a foreigner and dismiss me as merely half-witted, not sacrilegious.

At seven that evening Vien's aunt tapped on my door and said, 'Come down, party.' Wonderful words I always respond to. Downstairs the two French and two American men who were the long-term boarders, were seated at the table that had been set up in the middle of the living room. I asked them what the shindig was in aid of – I presumed that one of them must be leaving, or having some kind of celebration. But they said, 'It's just because it's Sunday.' Apparently my wonderful family gave a free feed to their guests each Sunday. The family did not join in. They lined up on the couch and got their pleasure from watching us eat. I was totally floored. A marvellous spread of food and unlimited amounts of beer appeared up as the family made us welcome, waited on us and fussed over us, constantly re-filling our plates and glasses and even adding the luxury of ice to our drinks. I closed my mind to the visions of typhoid that arose with the sight of great lumps of cracked ice being dumped in my beer. Earlier I had seen the ice-man delivering a mini iceberg. It had arrived wrapped in an old sack on the back of his bike and had then been smashed into smaller bits on the ground. It's not just on the basis of hygiene that I object to big lumps of ice in my beer – it severely interferes with its taste and potency.

The windows of my room had no flyscreens. I watched the mozzies come pouring in that night and worried about not having any anti-malarial tablets left. The next day I bought some incense coils and decided to try for some tablets at one of the hospitals. It was also a way of satisfying my curiosity. When Vien asked me where I wanted to go I replied, 'The Hospital in Chinatown, Cholon.' I had read in my guide book that it had a special clinic for foreigners. Uncle found me a cyclo, 'My brother,' he said.

It was a long but pleasant ride to Cholon. Being pedalled along and fanned by a slight breeze under the trees by the side of the road was not hard to bear. I was happily reclining in my cyclo at some stop lights, when out of the corner of my eye I saw something bright slide up beside me. I turned my head to behold a coffin! And a bicycle mounted coffin at that. Almost touching my shoulder, it was painted a brilliant red and was much gilded and decorated. I wondered if it was occupied.

Inside the hospital there were acres of empty, sterile-looking tiled floors. I asked directions of a nurse wearing a white cotton pant suit and an old-fashioned waitress's hat that had a turned up front and a gathered elastic back to constrain her hair. She took me to an office where someone wrote down the name of the clinic. I sallied forth and waved this piece of paper at everyone I encountered until I landed at the right spot.

The clinic was on the tenth floor. The lift lady waited until the elevator was full before she took off. A very commendable conservation of energy, it also gave the passengers plenty of time to examine each other. 'Place for Treatment for Persons from Other Countries' (not foreigners, I noted), the sign declared. The waiting room was a row of chairs on an open balcony that was only enclosed by a waist high railing. I hoped none of the customers was in need of psychiatric help. I felt ill just looking at the city-scape far below under my feet.

I was soon attended by a cordial male doctor who wrote me a script for the tablets I requested after much consultation backwards and forwards between me and the pharmacopoeia. When I asked how much I should pay him, he said, 'No charge. You were not sick and I have not treated you.'

Downstairs in the hospital grounds I located the pharmacy. They did not have the tablets, but directed me to the opposition, a private chemist shop across the road. I went to a side entrance gate. It was padlocked and the guard stationed there had to produce a key to let me through. The chemist did not have the pills either. He said they were not available in Vietnam. I returned to the doctor. He altered the script and I went through the process again. The hospital pharmacy did not have the tablets, so I crossed the road again. The guard looked at me askance as he unlocked the gate once more. I don't know what he thought I was playing at. The private chemist didn't have the pills either, but he said, 'Wait, I will go and get them.' I was given a tall, rickety stool to perch on and the chemist thundered off on his motorbike. While I waited, the assistant told me about her brother who now lives in Adelaide. It seemed everyone in Saigon had a relative in Australia. Soon the chemist returned with the goods. Hooray! Then I got the bill.

On the way back from the hospital I stopped at the Cholon Chinatown market. Former home of opium dens,

Cholon is big and alive and had gold galore, as well as mountains of jade jewellery. Hopping into another cyclo I went to eat at the Sinh Sin café, another travellers' hangout which is close to Kym's. In Saigon some one-way streets are forbidden to cyclos and pushbikes. My cyclo took a short cut down one of these because laws, as we all know, were meant to be broken. I had the novel, but unappealing experience of being pushed feet first into the opening of a one-way street and finding myself at a stop sign at the other end facing a solid, massed phalanx of motorbikes all intent on killing me. I shut my eyes and prayed.

By the time I had finished dinner it was dark and no cyclo was in sight, so I set off for my guest-house on foot. With my handbag clutched tightly under my arm and my umbrella furled, I was ready to defend myself. Muggers were not going to get my goodies easily or without a struggle. They would have to take me with the handbag. At the first corner I went off in the wrong direction and got lost. I found myself stumbling over rough, broken ground and rubbish in an unlit street that I did not know. Then I felt old vegetables under foot and I remembered that the extreme end of my street ended in a produce market. I had unwittingly entered the right street the wrong way. No traffic came through here. The market, a simple place where people spread their wares on the ground on sacks or in baskets and squatted by them against a wall, was spread over the entire street. I floundered on to where a few sellers still operated by the glow of kerosene lamps. I was pleased to find any light. I ploughed through the market and, although I felt very much out of place, I did not feel threatened.

I became aware of an unusual noise ahead of me. Nearing its source, I discovered that it was a brass band playing dance music. For a moment I thought I was hallucinating. A brass band seemed a highly unlikely commodity to find in a place like this. But soon I was marching along behind the band among the big mob of people it gathered as it slowly progressed up the street. Close up I could see that the band was the full catastrophe! It comprised a gigantic, shining tuba as well as trombones, trumpets, drums and musicians in smart caps and uniforms, who looked like the Salvation Army on parade.

Leaving this grand celebration, which was possibly a funeral, I continued on until I finally found the entrance to my alley. It was a warm night and all along this end of the street people had made themselves comfortable outdoors, cooking, eating, drinking or just sitting. As I walked into the alley, I could hear at least six different televisions and radios playing. The alleys were always full of noise and life, especially at night. And everyone's life here was an open book. In the evening, men sat smoking on rattan couches, little children ran around playing and women nursed babies while cats, dogs and chooks foraged for food among their feet.

During the day and evening the house I lived in was never quiet. It was open to all and sundry and there was always music, laughter, singing and talking. And day or night the echoing bells of hawkers on bicycles, or with two baskets suspended on shoulder poles, rang up and down the alleys. All day I could hear the bird on the balcony next door, who lived his entire life in a small cage. Whenever he saw me he would call louder and I would talk to him. Bored out of his brain, poor little bird, he would then chirp happily back to me.

The entire façade of the house was completely uncovered to the alley by day. From its four metre frontage you stepped directly into a foyer that housed the family's bikes and motorbikes. At night the house was enclosed by pulling a latticed wire grill across the alley front. Most of the surrounding houses were of the same design and in almost all of them the glow of a red lamp shining in front of an altar where incense burned before offerings could be seen. In the cool front rooms or the alley outside was where families lived – in public.

The living area of my house was a long, narrow space that had three large glassless windows covered by metal grilles in each side wall. A big 1960s vinyl couch and two matching armchairs with marvellous wooden arms stood on the tiled floor and wonderful wooden furniture was crammed shoulder to shoulder against all the walls. It was like living in an antique shop. At any time of the day I would be likely to find various members of the family asleep on the large wooden bed with only a sheet covering its board base. The feeling of being in a shop was further enhanced by the dishes, plates and vases that were packed solid, layer upon layer, on every level surface of the furniture. The most spectacular ornaments the room boasted were two stupendous Ching dynasty vases that loomed from the top of a carved chest. They shared their perch with two ponderous brass vases and three censors which were flanked by a pair of massive brass candle sticks. Stationed beside the phone in one corner was a lovely old wardrobe that was used as a notice board; numbers and messages were chalked on its front. A beautiful antique wooden-cased sessions clock hung on the wall. It was always an hour slow and it struck eleven for eight, but it was still going after 200 years. Several gaudily framed paintings decorated the walls, but the position of honour was given to a large picture of Uncle Ho. The altar with its red lamp, incense and offerings of fruit and flowers, reposed in a prominent corner facing the doorway.

The kitchen was a small, tiled space behind the living room where the family sat cross-legged on the floor to prepare and eat food. And well you might eat off their floor! It was continually being washed and no shoes came inside the house. The windows and doors of the living room and kitchen opened into a narrow passageway whose wall was the side of the neighbour's house. Cooking was done against the wall in the open air on a coal burning brazier and a tap over a shallow trough in the tiled floor constituted the wash house. Here dishes, clothes, children – and probably big people too – were sluiced down and cleaned up.

The family was extended and elastic. There were children, nephews, nieces, aunts, uncles and parents. A nephew, who was a university student, was the only member of the family with enough English for a conversation. One uncle was deaf and he had a deaf wife with a lovely, middle-aged face. The deaf uncle, although he spoke only with his hands, was very chatty. He talked more than the rest of the family put together and managed to communicate better with me than the non-English speakers. There was also a deaf mute child, a smiling girl with a constantly questioning look. The matriarch, Grandma, saved her false teeth for best. She never wore them in the mornings, only putting them in after lunch.

A tiny corkscrew metal staircase spiralled upwards to my room from the foyer in the front of the house. Some evenings I climbed up to the floor above me to talk to the fellows who lived there. Sitting under the shade of a big umbrella, on their charming tiled balcony, I would watch the sun set over the roof tops.

After a while I learned when it was time to shut my windows against the evening's mozzie invasion. At dusk the smell of incense would waft into my room from the balcony of the house across the alley where an altar perched on a small stand. During the day the altar always had fresh flowers on it, and every evening joss sticks were lit. The balcony of the house adjoining mine was a rough lean-to that had been tacked on level with my room. It touched the roof of the house across the alley and the residents used to reach over and put their face washers and towels and their baskets of chillis and other vegetables, on the roof to dry in the sun. A permanent clothes-line ran the length of the balcony and I often looked up to see someone sitting, only a few feet away among the washing, eating their noodles and smiling at me.

There were some minor detractions: the electric power usually went off for an hour or two during the day, and I was sometimes woken in the middle of the night by next door's dog routing imaginary burglars, or the neighbourhood cats having a sing-song on the roof. And the neighbour's rooster had a faulty time mechanism. He not only crowed loud and long at day break, but at nine in the evening too!

One day I accidentally ended up at the War Crimes museum. In Vietnam I was often glad that I was not an American, but at this museum I cringed to think that Australia had been involved in the American War too. I had been trying to get to the Museum of Natural History, but the War Crimes Museum seemed to be the place that other tourists wanted to go, so the cyclo riders presumed that I did too. Or did they take me there on purpose to shame me? It worked. The American army did some horrible things in Vietnam, and the museum contained photographs of them doing it; and smiling and enjoying it. I know that crimes and atrocities were committed on both sides, but only South Vietnamese and American evils were pictured. I found the museum experience extremely traumatic. I was shocked almost to tears by what I saw. Apart from the massacre of innocent people, the senseless destruction of the forests and the land was appalling. It also made me realise that I was probably eating agent orange every day that I spent in Vietnam. Seventy-five million litres of defoliant were sprayed and 2.2 million hectares were defoliated. Two million civilians were killed, as were 1,350,000 soldiers in the North and South, approximately 64,000 Americans and 423 Australians. At the height of the war 1.2 million tonnes of bombs were dropped in 400,000 air attacks each year at a cost of fourteen billion dollars.

The grounds of the museum housed a Huey helicopter, an A37 plane, a menacing seven ton bomb, a tank and a guillotine that had harvested heads, first for the French and then for the Diem regime in the South. There was also a replica of the tiger cages used to punish prisoners in Southern detention camps. All of them were sickening illustrations of man's inhumanity to man. The display inside the buildings included latter-day atrocities of the west, such as heavy metal music.

Another day I tried again to go to the Natural History Museum. I pointed it out on my map to the cyclo rider but, surprise, surprise, once more I ended up at the War Crimes Museum. On the footpath outside it I met Nigel from the Hanoi-Danang train again and we arranged to meet for dinner at Kym's.

Cyclo riders would sometimes rip off tourists if they got the chance. Who could blame them? They are so poor and they think that we are all rolling in cash and it doesn't matter to us. But you could get one who would look after you. Once I stopped to buy a coconut and the seller asked me for 3000 dong. My cyclo rider argued with him that the price was 2000 and that he shouldn't cheat me. It seemed that if they decided you were their property, they took care of you.

Another time I negotiated a cheap price for the trip back to my guest-house. The rider had insisted that it was a long way and when I got there I realised that it had been a lot further than I had thought. I said, 'It *was* a long way,' and gave him twice the fare. He nearly fell off his bike with shock, but he was pleased. The next day I came across him again. You couldn't help but get known to them, we westerners stick out like country lavatories among the neat Vietnamese. When I met yesterday's cyclo rider again outside the post office. I said, 'How much to Cholon?' and he replied, 'Oh, with you there is no problem. You will give me what is right.' And from then on we saw a good deal of each other, to our mutual satisfaction. He took me to places I needed to find but had no directions for and often found me shops where people gave me better deals than the regular tourist places. Nye was, like so many Vietnamese I met, a genuine and friendly person.

I finally got to the Natural History Museum on my third try. Well, I was actually taken to the zoo, but it was next door. I had to pay 10,000 dong to see both the museum and the zoo, so I was obliged to get my money's worth. For a person who doesn't like to see anything in a cage, I had done a lot of zoo-going lately.

The museum was dark ochre in colour and looked like a cross between a pagoda and a temple. Inside it was very grand and decorated in an eastern style. Among the exhibits was some antique porcelain, but it was mostly Chinese. Regrettably I saw few good pieces in Vietnam. The best collections are in Jakarta and Taiwan.

In the grounds of the museum, which were also the botanical gardens, I rested on a comfortable stone bench under one of the great trees that stood on the grass. At one time these were the best botanical gardens in Asia and they were still enjoyable. There were small trees contained in large urns, little formal gardens that were spanned by willow bridges and pretty, wing-roofed stone pagodas with stairs on their four sides that were guarded by seated stone lions. It was Saturday and courting couples and families with children strolled the paths, but it was not crowded.

In the zoo, the animals were enclosed in various pens. A large beautiful space was allotted to a couple of dozen ibis, who seemed perfectly content among masses of trees and a stream that ran through mock mountains. The monkey cage was an enormous nineteenth century wonder; a lofty edifice of wrought-iron domes that were open to the sky and in which big trees had been left growing for the monkeys to climb. This prison did not look nearly as bad as that of the big cats who were crammed into minute spaces. The elephants, poor things, were all chained; the big ones in a cage and three young ones in a row outside. A couple of beautiful big black panthers, some bears and the exotic birds had the worst of it. They were all incarcerated two or three to small cages.

I appreciated the food, prices and service at Kym's even more after I had been downtown and discovered the tourist ghetto that surrounds the expensive hotels. Walking along the High Street in this downtown tourist area, it was hard to pass some of the pathetic beggars. But some of the young women had the look of professionals. The first time an old lady held out her hat to me as I went by, I thought she was trying to sell it to me and walked on. It only hit me later that she had wanted help.

Outside one restaurant window I came upon a little boy of no more than six years old, who was hopefully pressing his box of Wrigley chewing gum up against the glass and trying to entice someone to come out and buy a packet. I sat on the window ledge and bought a couple. The wee one had a card pinned to his diminutive chest. It assured the world that he was a legitimate orphan and as such was entitled to support himself in this trade. Almost everywhere I went, beguiling tots flashed their Orphan Permits at me and sold me Wrigleys chewing gum. By the time I left Vietnam I had purchased enough gum to stock a shop.

One day I asked one of the little girls who sold postcards outside the post office why she wasn't in school. I thought that she was playing the wag, but she replied that she had no money to pay for school.

In the shops of the high street you could buy all the consumer items you could possibly want, and more. I found things that I had not been able to get for love or money in China. And in this country where so many people didn't have enough to eat, or were actually starving and many didn't have work, merchandisers were trying to convince the populace that they needed air fresheners, toilet cleaners and all kinds of useless junk.

I saw some funny things on a few of Saigon's many motorbikes. The Vietnamese could get up to four people on a bike. Sometimes children were placed on the handle bars, or on the petrol tank, and sometimes mother and father would ride with a child between them, as well as one in front of father. One day I was stopped in my tracks by a classic sight; a man steering a motorbike with one hand while he cradled a sleeping baby under the other arm. Another time I saw a young couple who were obviously in love. He was driving, she was riding pillion, but they were holding hands. Ladies driving, or riding pillion, protected their skin by wearing the kind of long, above the elbow, coloured cotton gloves that we would wear with a formal ball-gown.

I read that Hanoi and Saigon have the highest traffic accident death rate in the world. Once I saw the tangled wreck of a motorbike lying on its side in the middle of the road with one pathetic sandal underneath it. I shuddered. No one walked away from that. Crossing the street in peak hour traffic was also not without its dangers. I would get to the middle, breathe a sigh of relief that I had made it this far with all the legs and arms that I had left the curb with. Then, lulled into a false sense of security, I would suddenly be shocked out of my tranquillity by a blast, a screech and a rush of air as a motorbike came at me on the wrong side of the road!

One day my lovely inn keeper handed me a written invitation to her daughter Leung's thirteenth birthday party. I was stunned, Vien only looked twenty herself. I asked Emile, one of the Frenchman who lived upstairs, taught French at the university and spoke Vietnamese, to interpret for me so that I could ask her where I might have an *ou dai* made to wear to the party. She whizzed me to the market on her motorbike to buy the material. The Ben Thanh market, with its distinguishing central clock tower and pill boxes on each corner, has been Saigon's largest market for eighty years. Standing in the centre of a square where eight streets converge, it is a phenomenal place with a great variety of merchandise; bunches of frogs with their legs tied together, live squawking hens, baskets crammed with pig's snouts and ears, clothes, jewellery, dress material, kitchenware. It took hours to get all the way around the goods.

Outside the market a line of monks stood with their begging bowls in front of them. A tiny, ancient monk, who was obviously the elder, was in the fore. I said, 'Good morning, grandfather,' as I contributed to his bowl. To my surprise he said, 'Good morning, madame.'

The next day Vien took me around the corner of the alley to a dressmaker, and I got myself equipped with a pale blue outfit much to the delight of the populace, who took it as a tremendous complement that I liked their national dress enough to wear it. The *ou dai* usually does nothing for frumpy westerners who squash themselves into it, because it is intended only for slim and graceful Vietnamese women. I, at least, am slim.

Downstairs all day on Sunday a dozen women worked frantically cooking and preparing food. At the party only the men and the foreigners sat at the big round table to eat. The women served. The food and beer flowed freely. I was photographed with everyone possible, but especially the birthday girl, who was done up like a sore thumb with make-up and curls, and wore clumpy Doc Martins.

13 Snake Livers and Jungle Juice

The weather seemed to me to be getting more humid daily as the northeast monsoon, and Christmas, approached. Hoping to find a ship that was sailing in the direction of home, I canvassed the maritime shipping companies which fronted the Saigon River. Everyone I spoke to was unfailingly polite to me, but I could see that they all thought I was deranged; tourists travelled by aeroplane, not cargo or coastal boats. The manager of one company did say that a cruise ship was coming into port soon and he gave me the address of the firm that handled it. I shot around there only to find that the ship was going the other way – to Hong Kong and China.

There were flotillas of boats on the busy river that runs through Saigon's city centre – small boats that sailed the local waters and big cargo ships that went everywhere – but none carried passengers except the ferry to Cambodia. I wanted to go to Cambodia very much. There was, however, a slight draw-back to this venture. The area in the south where the ship would drop me was infested with Khmer Rouge guerillas, and travellers had been kidnapped and murdered there recently. And getting from the coast to Phnom Phen also entailed passing through dangerous country that was held by the Khmer Rouge. I considered risking it, but long-term foreign residents of Vietnam who had been to Cambodia via the northern route strongly advised me not to go to the south, so I reluctantly decided

223

against it. Giving up on ships, I considered the other possibilities. Qantas flew to Australia. That settled it.

I stopped to rest by the riverside, a pleasant place that is well supplied with chairs, benches, umbrellas and shade trees, and watched children swimming and playing in the river as I drank the milk from a coconut. They seemed oblivious to the grotty appearance of the water and the fact that it was littered with rubbish. A little way down-stream a hideous floating hotel had been sited on the bank. Up and down the water plied legions of sampans that were always manned by women, some of whom accosted tourists and offered to take them for a ride. One of these women sat down beside me. I eventually convinced her that I did not want an excursion on the water and tried to tell her what I did need. She could not understand toilet, or WC, so I drew a picture of a what I imagined looked like a loo. Apparently it didn't. Finally she got the message and taking me by the hand, led me off. Hauling me along the riverbank, she stopped here and there to chat and proudly exhibit me to her friends. They must have asked her where she was taking this strange woman and she made a gesture of pulling her pants down that I deduced must be sign language for what I wanted. We walked miles to that toilet and when we got there it was closed for renovations!

I found few public toilets in Vietnam and they all had a guardian who demanded an entry fee. The only decent one I came across was the one next to the post office in Saigon and it was, at 500 dong, also the cheapest. If you couldn't afford that, you went in the street. There was, however, blatant sexual discrimination in this practice. Although men urinated everywhere, women did not.

A wide street on which hotels and other imposing buildings were located ran along one side of downtown Saigon's riverbank. On the opposite bank a green park flourished until it petered out, at the edge of the inner city area, into the most deplorable cardboard and packing case shanties that tottered, decrepit and shonky, on stilts over the river.

One day I took a cyclo to the Ben Thanh market. I wandered along, stopping now and then to look at my map. Every time I did this, someone came and looked over my shoulder. While I was walking through a park opposite the market, a couple of wild-looking women who resembled gypsies came close to me and, pressing against me, pretended to help me read my map. Suddenly I felt threatened. My instincts told me to get away from these women and I started moving off. They said, 'Yes, yes, down here,' and attempted to lead me. I was trying to lose them when they were joined by a young man. By then I was on one of the broad main streets, the women were on one side of me and the young man on the other, at the gutter's edge.

I was holding my handbag firmly under my arm, but my purse was in my hand. I usually did this deliberately to deflect interest from my bag. Then, as one woman distracted my attention for a second, the other suddenly snatched the purse out of my hand and they both ran off. But I hadn't been looking where they had wanted me to and I saw that the purse had been thrown to the man, who shot off in the opposite direction. The ploy was for me to follow the women, but I reacted instantly without thinking and leaped after the man. They didn't call me the Greyhound at school for nothing. In a few yards I caught him and grabbing him by the shirt-front, shrieked, 'Give me back my purse, you bastard!' He threw it at me and broke away. Now I was really angry. Thinking, He's not bloody-well going to get away with that, I sprinted after him, seized him again and started hitting him over the head with my umbrella. He cried, 'Ow and oh', and put his arms over his head trying to protect himself, while I made a terrible fuss, yelling at him and calling him frightful names. Although there were a few people around, no one came to my aid. I suppose they could see that I wasn't being hurt. But no police appeared. The locals just stared at us open-mouthed.

I rushed into a nearby hotel thinking that they would call the cops. I said, 'Help, police, quick.' After fifteen minutes the combined efforts of the three desk staff managed to locate the number in the phone book, but the police wouldn't come. They said I had to go down to the station. The manager told me it wasn't far, 'About twenty minutes walk, no problem.' I said, 'What's the point.' I'd had time to cool down and consider the consequences. I had heard that the police either end up fining *you* or make a lot of trouble for you. I decided not to risk it. Anyway, the thief had only managed to take a handful of dong from my purse before I caught him. But I learned another lesson from this trauma. I had believed that being in a main street at half past eleven in the morning when there were people around made me safe.

I kept on walking until I found the Viet Cong Bank where I could change some more money. I needed it now. I didn't carry much local currency, everything was so cheap and I often used American dollars – safely hidden in a wallet that hung on a string around my neck under my clothes.

I was not having the most brilliant of days, so I was greatly relieved when my friend Nye, the cyclo rider, pedalled up, rescued me and took me home to my family to be comforted with tea and sympathy.

Everyone I met who had been in Saigon for some time had a tale of robbery to tell. Rene, one of the inmates of my guest house, told me how he had had his pocket picked by two enchanting female children who did not come up to his kneecaps. They were, however, just the right height to get at the pocket on the leg of his trousers and adroit enough to overcome the difficulty of its secure zip fastening. Brian had been done by the Dodgy Brothers Money Changers. He received a large stack of dong and waded through it, counting carefully. It was correct. Then someone, obviously an accomplice, went past and accidentally knocked his shoulder. He was twenty dollars short when he counted his money at home.

Later that week I went on a five-day tour of the Mekong delta. Once part of the Khmer Kingdom of Cambodia, this is the flat, lusciously green and beautiful southernmost part of Vietnam which the sediment from the mighty Mekong River system has made rich and fertile. One of the great rivers of the world and Asia's third longest after the Yangtze and the Yellow Rivers, Song Cuu Long, the River of The Nine Dragons, rises high in the Tibetan plateau to flow 4,500 kilometres through China, Laos, Cambodia and Vietnam to the South China Sea. At Vinh Long, the Mekong splits into several branches which are criss-crossed by countless canals and channels, some man-made and 1,500 years old. Half of the land mass of the delta is densely populated and under cultivation. There are 3,723,189 hectares of pineapples, bananas, coconut, sugar cane, other fruit and rice and large amounts of fish are caught here as well. The mangrove swamps and jungle further south are sparsely inhabited and it was from here that the Viet Minh resistance fighters fought the French, and the Viet Cong fought the United States in the American War.

On the morning of departure, taking my life in my hands once more, I let Vien deliver me by motorbike, bag and all, to the bus terminal. It had gone without me! After all the times I'd waited hours for transport that departed late, I had arrived dead on time to find that the bus had left. Everyone else had arrived, so they simply took off. No one at the office was concerned. I was squeezed into another bus, a tiny mini affair that was already packed to the brim. A few kilometres out of town we stopped at a hat factory where a tour had been arranged. But I was saved from this dubious pleasure. The guide said, 'No, no, not you. You go on other bus.' Reprieved, I was shunted onto the bus that was my rightful conveyance and which had just finished the awesome hat factory tour. Later I discovered that the people on this bus thought that I had hitched a ride. Greatly curious, they came up to me in ones and twos asking, 'How *did* you get onto our bus?'

It was a good thing I abandoned the other bus. Later that day we came upon it broken down on the side of the road. And although our driver spent a certain amount of time lying under it – an obligatory procedure that often seemed to work – in this instance it didn't and we left it and its unhappy occupants there.

The travellers on the still-functioning bus were a jolly bunch. There were eight rather gorgeous Israeli of mixed gender, two nice Australians, a Swedish couple and an American girl. I thought I would hate her when I first got on the bus – she did not stop talking for two hours straight – but in the end I quite liked her.

The roads we had begun making our way south on were not too good at the beginning of the trip, but once we hit the country roads they deteriorated badly. No lines were marked on these much repaired, bumpy paths and traffic drove all over the place. But the scenery was beautiful. Soon we began traversing rice paddies that were dotted with ancestral graves, crossed some immense rivers and drove alongside a great deal of water. It was everywhere. All the houses were surrounded by canals, and the villages were separated from the road by water that was spanned by all kinds of rough connections – a fallen log, a couple of planks, or a tiny, hand-built bridge. Now and then a lovely white ibis winged overhead or stood, mirrored in a water-logged field, posing gracefully.

After lunch we were frog-marched to a landing and onto a boat for a river tour. The boat was small and narrow with hard wooden plank seats on which we were crammed two abreast. We cruised along many water-ways at great length and the seats became harder and harder as time went by. But the territory we were in was like nowhere I had ever been before. It was a place of mysterious green shade where not much direct sunshine penetrated. I had the feeling that living here would be like existing in the depths of a rain forest. I could see little huts, some of them only shanties, on the edge of the water and I wondered what the people did. Nothing in the food line seemed to be growing here and it did not seem possible that there could be. There was so much water. Eventually we came to an area where the rain forest scenery ended and almost impenetrable jungle began. This was where the Viet Cong had hidden during the war. They had chosen this region because it had been uninhabited then and it was still pretty much deserted. Our guide said that nothing grew here as the soil was poor. He made us get out and walk. I could not see a foot in front of me through the jungle. Without the guide I would never have found my way out, or seen the booby traps and the hiding places he showed us: metal trapdoors covered with earth which you lifted with a piece of string or wire. There were also bunkers built under low mounds of vegetation where the Viet Cong had hidden during the day. At night they used to go into the villages.

We came to a place at the water's edge where a series of tall sticks stuck out of the water close to the shore. They were there to let everyone know not to land. Hanging from the tops of the sticks were pieces of reed attached to strings that connected to hand grenades. Our guide told us that they were warnings that said, 'Keep off. This is our place.' He also showed us how the local people set traps for mongoose and rats. Everything was made from natural materials, so there was no litter.

Having survived the jungle trek, we tramped back to our boat and moved to a populated area where people grew produce, mainly fruit such as longans. I liked the bath house arrangements that were built over the water behind the dwellings. And I loved the pig pens made entirely of bamboo which had slatted floors and stood on stilts over the stream.

Our guide took us to a place in one village that he called a factory, but was a hut with a rammed earth floor on which two women were weaving sleeping mats on a frame. Then we hiked a great way through a garden where flowers, bonsai plants, and pine trees were grown commercially.

Then, after a cheap and tasty *baguette* – a Vietnamese torpedo-shaped, crusty bread roll filled with choice bits and pieces – from a street stall, it was back on the bus once more to drive into a spectacular pink sunset that was etched with the black outlines of coconut palms and reflected in the still waters of the rice paddies.

Just on dusk we were held up at the site of a bad road smash. A motorbike was crumpled on the side of the road and directly under my window sprawled a dead body. Lying on his back with one leg bent under him and a pool of blood fanning out from his head, the deceased man's bloody face looked up at me. The bare skin of his torso was an un-natural yellow and there was no movement of his chest. The dead man lay all alone. No one covered him or came near. I was the only one who seemed to see him. There were no police or ambulance in attendance. Another limp body was being man-handled into a cyclo like a sack of flour, while a crowd stood around and stared. The bus had to wait quite a while for the traffic jam to clear and all this time I looked down on the abandoned corpse.

It was dark by the time we got on the 'fairy' that transported us across the vast expanse of the Mekong River to Can Tho, 169 kilometres south of Saigon, for the night. Everyone was put off the bus to hike onto the ferry except me. I think the driver had got the message that I wasn't all that keen on walking. When the others climbed down he turned to me and said, 'No, okay you stay.'

The hotel in Can Tho, passable downstairs but a real dive above, was the worst place I stayed in Vietnam. To add insult to injury, I had to pay an extra three dollars to have a room to myself. I was very glad I had invested in this luxury when I saw that all the rooms had double beds. I did not fancy hopping into bed with some female, or even a bloke that I did not know, as the other single travellers had to do. The hotel had no hot water or electric plugs and although I had previously thought that I had experienced the ultimate in rock hard pillows, those of Can Tho took the prize. But there was a marvellous mosquito net over my big double bed. It took, however, a lot of manoeuvring and swearing to get it up and assembled on all its little hooks.

Our merry band of wanderers trooped down to the bus like Good Little Tourists and were taken to a restaurant, where we were shunted upstairs for dinner. It was more secluded on the second floor, but it was much hotter – and so were the prices. The Israeli contingent and I did an exodus and went next door, to an outdoor café.

I had a delicious omelette washed down by a large bottle of beer. Then I decided to go off on my own to the market to buy a pair of shoes. I got lost and didn't ever find the market, instead I found a street of shops. I bought a pair of shoes for four dollars. I was still lost, so I produced the hotel card I'd had the sense to ask for after my unforgettable experience in China. Sent in the right direction several times, I got lost again and went into a shop to ask for help. A small girl took me by the hand and towed me around the streets and delivered me personally to the hotel. In the doorway she announced me, the translation of which probably ran something like, 'Look what I found. Here is one of your stupid tourists who got lost.' It was the ultimate indignity to be hand-delivered by a pint-sized know-all with a superior attitude.

I was up at the crack of dawn, courtesy of the propaganda machine that started business at five outside my window. The guide also smashed on my door at six and told me to get up. After a good breakfast at a sidewalk café next to the hotel, I waited half an hour for the bus.

We set off again and drove thirty-two kilometres south to the village of Phung Hiep, passing a snake farm along the way. I asked where all the snakes came from and the guide said that they were caught locally. Soon afterwards some of the group asked for a toilet. The guide told us, 'I will stop the bus and you can go in the bushes.' Not on your Nelly, I thought. I was convinced that I had done the right thing when we got to the main street of Phung Hiep and found a very active live snake market in progress. All along the roadside countless furiously arching and whipping reptilian specimens were displayed for sale in wire netting enclosures. Cobras raised their hoods and hissed at me and writhing, deadly poisonous green mambas eyed me with menace as I walked past. I stopped to admire lines of tall racks on which dangled row after row of small round objects like nuts that were attached by strings in artistic arrangements. They turned out to be snake livers that had been hung up to dry. It was very good to eat snake liver, I was told.

Then it was back on the bus again to a floating market where an armada of sampans sold all manner of goods and services from hair cuts to coffins. An example of what the boat offered, such as pineapples or bananas, hung like a flag on a pole above it. There was even a floating bar, a sampan filled with brightly labelled bottles.

Later we climbed into another boat and cruised along more canals, waterways and channels until we were again deep in another part of the delta. Everywhere we went we were greeted with shrieks of joy and choruses of waves and hellos. Waving back, I began to feel like Queen Elizabeth on a royal tour. Stepping ashore at one small compound, we were taken to visit a family home on the riverbank. The house was only half enclosed and much of the family's living was done outside, under a canopy of big trees, in an elfin green gloom that felt like being underwater. The occupants of the house fed us pomelos, pineapple, bananas and jack fruit, as well as goodies made from coconut milk, fruit and rice that were wrapped in banana leaves. I tried the home-brewed rice wine that was offered. It tasted like brake fluid and was not terribly well received by my stomach.

After several hours on the water, we were marched in crocodile file back onto the bus, taken across the Mekong on the ferry and progressed to Vin Long where we were shown a huge, and I mean *huge* pair of snakes. These hefty fellows were a mated pair of pythons that were about five metres long and so heavy that I could not lift the female off the ground. No one else, except a couple of local two-year-olds for whom Ms Python was no big deal, would even touch her.

Back in Saigon the bus dropped us at Kym's café where I bought a beer for the driver and the guide and collected a monetary reward for them from the other passengers. The amount I was able to extract from our generous mob was minute, but the two men thanked me profusely. Their wages were only four dollars a day, I discovered.

I wheeled home to Vien's in a cyclo in the cool evening air to be received like a long lost family member returning from a distant voyage. Then I had to sit down and tell everyone about my adventures.

The next morning I asked Vien to drop me at a gold shop on her way to the market. I wondered why she hung around watching as I stepped up to the counter. Then she called me over and said, 'Lydia, Lydia, come, this is not good for you.' She must have known something that I did not. I got back on the motorbike and Vien took me to another shop where I disposed of almost the last of my dong in readiness to leave the country.

The Qantas staff had told me that the only available ticket to Adelaide was via Bangkok and Melbourne. They told me that the plane left at half past one, explained how long I would spend in Bangkok and gave me the time I would arrive in Melbourne. When I went to collect my ticket, two young women told me again that I went via Bangkok, how long I stayed there and what time I left. But this time I was told that the plane left at five past three. 'How long does it take to get to Bangkok?' I asked. The two girls exchanged blank looks. Then a bloke wandered up from the back of the shop and said, 'Can I help you. I've just come from America to do some work here.' He looked at my ticket and said, 'You are flying direct to Melbourne.' I said, 'No I'm going via Bangkok.' 'No no,' he said, 'This is a through ticket.' I read the ticket. The departure time was twenty past four. This man then took me aside and said, 'I'm here to straighten out a few problems.' I said, 'I think you are very much needed.'

One of my extended family was summoned to drive me to the airport. I loved the car that was produced for the purpose: a tiny, ancient, but lovingly hand-painted Renault.

On the way to the airport we passed a Buddhist funeral. Not another omen, I hoped. There were gongs, drums, a band, a float with a dragon on it and monks waving burning incense who walked in front of the ornate coffin that was borne on the shoulders of the male relatives. This was the way to go.

At the airport check-in counter I was asked if I wanted my luggage sent direct to Sydney. 'Why should I would want it to go there?' I asked. 'Because that's where your ticket is for,' was the reply. 'And then on to Adelaide?' I said. 'No only to Sydney.' It took an hour and the regional manager of Qantas to sort out this little hiccough, but in the end there was, after all, no stop off in Bangkok. The plane went via Singapore. But I was home for Christmas.